CW01501823

To Lara, Milo, Cassia and Theo

*The book none of you wanted, but understanding
I did, graciously supported its creation*

A More Perfect Union

Also by Marina Wheeler

The Lost Homestead:
My Mother, Partition and the Punjab

A More Perfect Union

THE EUROPE WE NEED

Marina Wheeler

WEIDENFELD & NICOLSON

First published in Great Britain in 2025 by Weidenfeld & Nicolson,
an imprint of The Orion Publishing Group Ltd
Carmelite House, 50 Victoria Embankment
London EC4Y 0DZ

An Hachette UK Company

The authorised representative in the EEA is Hachette Ireland,
8 Castlecourt Centre, Dublin 15, D15 XTP3,
Ireland (email: info@hbgi.ie)

1 3 5 7 9 10 8 6 4 2

Copyright © Marina Wheeler 2025

The moral right of Marina Wheeler to be identified as
the author of this work has been asserted in accordance
with the Copyright, Designs and Patents Act of 1988.

All rights reserved. No part of this publication may be
reproduced, stored in a retrieval system, or transmitted
in any form or by any means, electronic, mechanical,
photocopying, recording, or otherwise, without the
prior permission of both the copyright owner and the
above publisher of this book.

A CIP catalogue record for this book is
available from the British Library.

ISBN (Hardback) 978 1 3996 3724 4
ISBN (Ebook) 978 1 3996 3726 8
ISBN (Audio) 978 1 3996 3727 5

Typeset by Input Data Services Ltd, Bridgwater, Somerset

Printed in Great Britain by Clays Ltd, Elcograf, S.p.A.

www.weidenfeldandnicolson.co.uk
www.orionbooks.co.uk

Contents

Author's Note   ix

Chapter One: Where We Are   1
Chapter Two: Eurovisions   29
Chapter Three: Ever Tighter   61
Chapter Four: Another Europe Is
    Possible   92

Bibliography   133
Acknowledgements   145
About the Author   147

Author's Note

EEC – EC – EU

The European project has gone through numerous iterations and name changes. What is now the European Union (EU) was originally the European Economic Community (EEC). It became the European Community (EC) by the Treaty on European Union 1992 (also known as the Maastricht Treaty).

Maastricht also created the European Union – which at that time covered other things as well. The Treaty of Lisbon (2007) later abolished the European Community, bringing all 'pillars' of activity under the umbrella of the European Union.

For ease of understanding, I have opted to refer to the European Union, the EU and EU law throughout except where the distinction between the EEC, the EC and the EU seems important. Some sources quoted use 'the Community' to refer to the EU or its earlier iterations, the EEC or EC.

The Treaties

The founding Treaty was the Treaty of Rome 1958. This was amended numerous times by the Single European Act (1986), the Treaty of European Union or Maastricht Treaty (1992), the Treaty of Amsterdam (1997), the Treaty of Nice (2001), and the Treaty of Lisbon (2007).

Before the Lisbon Treaty, a Constitutional Treaty was agreed, but after it was rejected by voters in France and the Netherlands, it was abandoned.

Lisbon settled the current treaty framework that governs the EU: the Treaty on European Union (TEU) and the Treaty on the Functioning of the European Union (TFEU).

Again, for ease of understanding, unless there is special need to identify a particular Treaty, I refer generically to 'the Treaty'.

The Courts

A word about the Courts.

The Lisbon Treaty renamed the judicial branch of the EU, the Court of Justice of the European Union (CJEU). This comprises both the higher Court, the European Court of Justice (ECJ) and the General Court – both based in Luxembourg. Throughout the text, however, I refer simply to the European Court of Justice (ECJ), as this is how it is most commonly referred to outside legal circles.

The European Court of Human Rights, based in Strasbourg, is part of the Council of Europe, not the EU. I refer to it either by its full name or as 'the Strasbourg Court'.

Federalism – Federalist

Federalism has different meanings depending on the context. In this book – in the context of the European project – federalism implies centralised EU governance with strong pan-European institutions and reduced decision-making at member state level. The ultimate goal of a Federal Europe would be a supranational European superstate.

'The truth comes as conqueror only because we have lost the art of receiving it as guest' Rabindranath Tagore, *The Fourfold Way of India*, 1924

Chapter One

Where We Are

Outside the Berlaymont building in central Brussels, only twenty-seven fluttering national flags remain. Standing with my former colleagues (now friends), one Irish, one Dutch, two streets up from where we used to work, we ponder the absence of the Union Jack. Masking an inner turmoil I don't quite understand myself, I contemplate how other traces of the departing British must have been expunged from the European Commission's headquarters. Photographs of the Queen, I imagine, went with the staffers. English survives. Now a global means of communicating, it is still an official Community language. But what about tea? Is there still an afternoon brew? Does the canteen still offer Earl Grey?

In the UK, too, reassuring old rituals are gone. No more footage of EU leaders arriving at summits, holing up in windowless rooms to negotiate hard into the night. No more breakfast communiqués allowing the press to report that, once again, crisis in Europe has been averted.

Long an overworked notion, 'crisis in Europe' has started to seem horribly real. In fact, very little in our world now seems safe. Geopolitically, say the experts, this is a perilous moment. Perhaps not an ideal time, some suggest, for the UK to have unmoored itself from a strategic bloc like the EU.

When did the sky turn so dark? It's hard to say precisely. One moment, China's opening up to the world heralded a 'Golden Era'. Delegations flew to Beijing in search of new business. David Cameron and Xi Jinping downed pints together, beaming to cameras. Then we blinked, and China had become the world's second-largest economy, aiming to take first place.

Through its Belt and Road Initiative, it sponsored huge infrastructure projects in overlooked parts of the globe, securing contracts for the supply of rare and essential minerals. Its 'wolf warrior' diplomacy set out to counter hostile US-led narratives. But were they just narratives? In Hong Kong, it crushed dissent with tear gas and rubber bullets, abandoning the commitment to 'one country, two systems'. In the South China Seas, new military bases appeared. The People's Liberation Army patrolled the waters. Unnerved, China's neighbours sought legal arbitration. It ignored the ruling.

Frantically, we decoupled our economy from this 'strategic competitor'. In a screeching U-turn, we extracted the tech-giant Huawei from UK telecoms. Discussions remain cordial, we co-operate where we can, but the golden age is no more. Universities and public bodies seek funding elsewhere. Chinese espionage is rife, we are told.

Meanwhile, US foreign policy pivoted to the Pacific. Aircraft carriers now monitored strategically vital passages, securing shipping and, America said, deterring aggression. We dutifully rewrote our own defence plans, committing our resources, not imagining that soon we might need them closer to home.

In February 2022, Russia began amassing troops on the Ukrainian border. Xi and Putin met and declared a 'no limits' strategic partnership between 'friends of steel'. Then tanks rolled into a country that we see as sovereign, but Russia does not.

A year later, with Russia still destroying cities and shelling civilians, the Chinese ambassador in Paris opined that none of the Baltic states had 'status' in international law, questioning the sovereignty, it seemed, not just of Ukraine but all the former Soviet Republics.

Putin's intentions aside, we wondered what this might tell us about China's intentions regarding Taiwan – the island to which the Kuomintang government fled after the 1949 Revolution, and which today manufactures most of the world's semiconductors. The question hovers, unanswered.

Russia's invasion of Ukraine was a flagrant breach of international law. But to Western consternation, many countries chose not to condemn it. Modi's India, a nuclear-armed, rising economic power, more populous than China, sits on the fence. The West's self-perception – our claim to a moral superiority – is viewed sceptically in much of the global south. Where we see principled action, they see hypocrisy and a partial application of the rules.

Donald Trump, re-elected to the presidency, is no fan

of rules and openly partisan, appearing to relish reversing the allegiances of his predecessors. In the Oval Office, President Zelensky of Ukraine faced a grilling, while an emollient approach appeared to be taken towards Vladimir Putin.

The 'America First' Trump administration is unsparing of its European allies. The UK currently provokes less ire than the EU. Whether this endures remains to be seen. As Russian missiles pounded Ukraine, Europeans were collectively chastised at the 2025 Munich Security Conference for alleged crimes against free speech.

Painful as some of the leaked epithets for us have been – 'pathetic', 'freeloaders' – they contain an element of truth. For too long we have relied on America's security umbrella. Even the French, who talk about 'strategic autonomy', have done little in practice to enhance Europe's military capability. Now it seems that Europe must take greater responsibility for its defence, while remaining – many of us hope – in a strong alliance with the US.

That's not all. Across Europe, the rise of illiberal political parties challenges national governments and hampers efforts to respond to Russia. Long a thorn in the side of the EU, Hungary's Viktor Orbán provides a playbook for others. There is, it seems, a creeping authoritarianism: a growing sympathy for the strongmen, a turning against migrants who arrive to make a new life. There may never have been a halcyon time when things felt comfortable and right, but one thing has become clear: few of us are quite where we want to be.

*

After a democratic vote in 2016, Britain left the European Union. In the pages to come, I will be very critical of the EU. This is tough love. I am explaining my view of what went wrong because I want to explore a better way. Inside or out, Britain and Continental Europe are still allies and friends. We could be friendlier – but friends tell friends the truth (as they see it). And, as the world gets increasingly dangerous, perhaps now more than ever we need the EU to work, for all our sakes.

Britain, an island with a long maritime history and global footprint, is also a European nation. Our history is shaped by Europe, and Europe's is shaped by ours. With five million settled European nationals living here, we remain a larger European nation than, say, Latvia. Although the EU's share of UK trade has been declining for years, the EU is still our largest trading partner. The special status of Northern Ireland – part of the UK but within the EU's single market for goods – is also a tie, albeit one that some people deeply regret. It matters greatly where our neighbours are headed.

Most of my life, I have cared about the European project. When the UK held its first referendum on membership, I was a child at the European School in Brussels. Later, back in Belgium, I took a master's degree in EU law and stayed on for three years to practise. It was then that I married Boris Johnson, whom I had known at school.

Boris was always a sceptic – which I was not. He was

a Conservative – which I was not. I enjoyed the difference, but come the 2016 referendum, our political views unexpectedly converged, for what felt like the first time ever.

Though I wasn't part of the campaign, the Vote Leave slogan 'Take Back Control' chimed with me. Mostly I observed – in an anthropological way – the goings-on. When invited, I took part in panels. If they wanted to hear my view, I thought I might as well give it. I wrote about sovereignty for the UK Human Rights Blog, and the *Spectator* picked up the article.

My stance prompted furious rows with some family members. One was unimpressed by what she called my 'micro-arguments'. Perhaps I sounded lawyer-ish. Others can find that annoying, a hazard of the job. But my point was a big one: membership of the EU, I felt, was undermining our democracy. My micro-arguments were the evidence I deployed to show I wasn't just conjuring up a position to be contrary.

Since divorcing Boris and being embraced back into the bosom of liberal friendships that had gone cool, I have had ample opportunity to recant. I have been given all manner of Euro memorabilia by friends who hope I will. I have ashtrays and mugs that are blue with yellow stars, a 'No Man Is an Island' tea towel. Almost every day at work, my colleague Martin watches me sip from the Euro-flag mug he gave me, hoping.

At this distance, my vision is clearer. I am no longer married to a politician. I am not party political and have no tribe. As a barrister, I know something of the law, but I also have insight into the media and politics.

In terms of identity, I have feet in different camps, too. My late mother was Indian and married my British journalist father, Charles Wheeler, when he was based in Delhi. I was born during his next posting to West Berlin, at the height of the Cold War, not long after the Berlin Wall was built and the Cuban Missile Crisis brought the world close to disaster. My early childhood was spent in the US. Called on to pledge allegiance to the American flag in Wednesday morning assembly, I would place my left hand on my heart, not the right. This was necessary, I thought, because I was British.

I was twelve when I first lived in the UK, so folklore about Nelson, Wellington and 'Our Island Story' passed me by. The pride I now feel in Britain comes largely from practising law. For many years I litigated for the government, defending claims for judicial review. It is a huge strength of our system that it faces its critics, entertaining challenges to its decisions. Of course it has flaws, but through trial and error, our imperfect democracy evolves.

Throughout my lifetime, I have also watched the European project evolve.

In 1973, Britain joined what was then the European Economic Community, and the BBC posted my father to Brussels as its chief Europe correspondent. Aged eight, I was plucked from my sunny little school in Washington DC and transported back to Europe on the SS *France*, flagship of the French Line. (Warned, as we boarded, not to get lost, I promptly did, racing eagerly around its sumptuous decks.)

Most pupils at the European School in Uccle, not least my classmate, Alexander Boris Johnson, had fathers who worked in the European institutions. Boris's father, Stanley, drafted water-quality directives in the Commission. Not coming from a Eurocrat family, my sister Shirin and I didn't strictly qualify for a place at the school, but my mother, Dip, twisted the headmaster's arm, promising to set up an English-language library in the school's new British section.

The posting lasted just a few years. Although broadly pro-European, my father found little positive to report about the EU. For a start, the visible side effects of subsidised farming were grotesque. The Common Agricultural Policy (CAP) fixed prices regardless of output. This inevitably led to massive overproduction: legendary lakes of unwanted wine and mountains of butter and beef. My father filed these stories until they were no longer news. (Less visibly, the surpluses were sold on world markets at subsidised rates, undermining the struggling agriculture of developing countries.)

After a referendum in 1975 confirmed British membership, the EU was no longer much of a story. Moves to reduce trade barriers were slow and it settled into a kind of torpor. In 1976, we moved to the UK.

When I came back to Brussels in the 1990s, however, the place had a buzzing new energy. New democracies in Spain, Portugal and Greece had joined. Communist regimes in the East were crumbling. Almost unbelievably, the Berlin Wall had come down. People in the West were energised by plans to liberalise European economies, to 'complete' the single market. At the time I wholeheartedly supported all this – so much so, in fact, that I had come back to Brussels to study EU law. I thought that by working to build Europe, I would help to make the world better.

Over time, however, bad policy choices – such as the way the euro was set up – dented this faith. Each year, more political decisions were taken far away – in Brussels, Strasbourg and Luxembourg – by politicians, bureaucrats, even judges we couldn't identify, let alone name. The connection with ordinary citizens was being stretched dangerously thin. Something that once worked well for the people of Europe (including, on balance, the British) had lost its way. By 2016, I felt that the EU had come to mistake its own interests for those of its citizens, and that this was a path we should not follow.

After the vote, people regularly shouted obscenities outside our house, aimed at Boris, who had been prominent in the Leave campaign. One evening, a small, less threatening-sounding crowd gathered on the street. Behind opaque glass panes I heard rustling. Then young voices, schoolboys perhaps, chanted, 'EU, we love you! EU, we love you!'

To the young people on my doorstep, I suspect that

the EU represented something modern and cosmopolitan, offering possibilities beyond our own shores. I understand the yearning, but I think the sentiment is misguided and treats Europe as the world. Many outside the EU see it as a regional block that chauvinistically protects its own.

Why *should* we have such a marked preference for twenty-seven nearby countries over all others, including those in the Commonwealth with which the UK has close historic ties? In his book *Eurowhiteness*, Hans Kundnani (born to a Dutch mother and Indian father) seeks to puncture the 'myth' of cosmopolitan Europe. He sees the EU's exclusivity as a regionalism 'analogous to nationalism . . . but on a larger, continental scale'. For every dismantled internal barrier, a reinforced external one is erected. 'Fortress Europe' is increasingly real.

Spain's southern border is actually in Morocco. There, a three-metre-high reinforced fence seals off the EU's affluent 'border-free zone' from outsiders, and protects Spain's colonial enclaves, Ceuta and Melilla. Walking the perimeter of the Berlin Wall is now a distant memory, but surveying this – a place where dozens of would-be migrants were killed in 2022 – vividly recalls it.

Who counts? Who matters? Who do we see as our own?

In the aftermath of the referendum, many who were close to the metropolitan levers of power were shocked to discover a swathe of people – 'Leavers' – whose experience of the world was quite different to theirs. For this comfortable demographic (my demographic), the free movement of people mostly meant easy access to the Continent, perhaps to a second home in Provence or the choice to relocate to edgy Berlin. It meant studying abroad. It meant a ready pool of reliable Polish gardeners, plumbers and builders.

For many others, whose wages were stagnant, who competed with newcomers for flats, GP appointments or local school places, large-scale migration felt like a threat. These people felt ignored and betrayed by politicians who made promises they knew they couldn't keep, not least about the numbers who would move to the UK.

The collapse of Communism in Eastern Europe was momentous, and 9/11 altered my immediate world. Even so, despite differing opinions, I didn't lose friends over these events. Leaving the EU was different: it was the most divisive political change I have lived through. Some friends said they woke up in a country they suddenly no longer liked. They were angry. Much of the establishment, dismayed by the vote, declared, 'We won't accept it. These Leavers are thick and they are racist. They were duped by lies.' In a darkening mood of suspicion and resentment, a kind of hysteria set in.

Some otherwise sensible people expected EU nationals would be rounded up and deported. Then, in late August, the BBC reported 'a frenzied racist attack triggered by the Brexit referendum'. The victim was a forty-year-old Polish man. Boris had become foreign secretary and I remember the diplomatic fallout lasting for months. The Polish ambassador went to Harlow to visit the scene of the crime. The Commission president, Jean-Claude Juncker, piled in. 'We Europeans,' he intoned in a state of the union address, 'can never accept Polish workers being beaten up, harassed or even murdered in the streets of Essex.'

At the trial, however, a murkier story emerged. Arkadiusz Jóźwik had been sitting on a wall in the late evening, eating takeaway pizza with two friends, when he got into a confrontation with a group of teenage boys on bikes. From behind the wall, one of them punched him on the back of the head. Jóźwik fell, hit his skull on the pavement and died in hospital two days later. There was no obvious motive. A witness said that Jóźwik had racially abused one of the boys, who wasn't white. There appeared to be no mention of Brexit. No matter the absence of evidence – in some people's minds this will remain 'the frenzied racist attack triggered by the Brexit referendum'.

A similar hostility became the rule on grander stages, too. The EU was always going to make sure that leaving was difficult – to deter others and play up the value of membership – but the level of emotion, the peevishness and spite, came as a surprise.

When Covid hit, the UK's vaccine taskforce acquitted itself well, supporting, selecting, then guiding administration of the first reliable vaccine of the pandemic. Together with Oxford University, AstraZeneca, an Anglo-Swedish company with a French chief executive, produced a working Covid jab that they offered to the world at cost price. Most of us in the UK gratefully received at least one shot of it. Yet the reaction from former partners – as the EU's own vaccine rollout hit trouble – was sour and contemptuous. In January 2021, Emmanuel Macron baselessly described the AstraZeneca jab as 'quasi-effective' in over sixty-fives. German regulators flip-flopped over its efficacy. Angela Merkel refused the jab in February, saying it wasn't approved for her age group, then she took it in April. The European press frequently referred to the Oxford–AstraZeneca vaccine as a cheap and inferior alternative to others on offer. Unsurprisingly, on the Continent, public confidence in it declined and available doses were unused, though this did not stop the Commission suing the company for allegedly under-supplying the EU. (Both sides ultimately claimed victory.)

With the passing of time, these animosities died down a little. Russia's invasion of Ukraine changed the dynamic between us and our Continental neighbours. Boris defiantly walking around Kiev with President Zelensky presumably rankled, but the UK's quick, decisive support helped to turn Britain from a pariah and object of derision back into a partner. And it underlined the seriousness of the common threats we face.

In light of these threats, the need to work together is urgent. But we are yet to find a way to do it that commands public support and respect. Keir Starmer's government claimed to have 'reset' relations with the EU, culminating in a summit in May 2025. Some declared what emerged to be a betrayal of Brexit, using colourful sex-slave analogies. Downing Street spun a line that 'Britain is back'. In reality, the agreement seemed to amount only to an agreement to agree, short on essential detail, with lofty advice not to worry. People can relax, seemed to be the message: this is a practical, sensible government that has left behind ideology and abstract hang-ups like national sovereignty. (Hang-ups such as seeing value in taking decisions for oneself.)

In short, Britain's European path is far from resolved. It feels like we are stumbling forward, the government gingerly testing what the public will take, one eye always on Reform UK. Some suspect that Starmer plans to inch back into the EU bit by bit. They haven't forgotten that, in an effort to stop the UK leaving at all, Labour – shepherded by Starmer – voted against Theresa May's doomed deal. They haven't forgotten that he campaigned for a second referendum, then said Labour was open to staying in the single market (however that was meant to work).

Personally, I don't think people should be forever held to a position they took in the past. But if you are leading the country, it seems fair to expect some basic clarity about what your position actually is and why you hold it. The government fears that Europe is a divisive topic and it hardly featured in the 2024 general election. Yet there are many ways in which our relationship with the EU might develop. We as citizens are entitled to know where this government thinks our national interests lie. No. 10 briefings through the press are not adequate. The world is in a precarious state. If, instead of talking frankly about the decisions we face, we keep our heads in the sand, we risk making poor choices and finding ourselves more divided than ever.

Start with democracy. Over the years, citizens have been consulted about the EU's direction on numerous occasions. Referenda in France, Ireland, Denmark and the Netherlands rejected steps to advance integration. The draft treaties were tweaked or repackaged, and the votes were rerun. Promises were made to make the EU more 'relevant' and bring it closer to the people. And yet, in almost every country across the Channel, discontent with established parties and the European project is rife. The extremes are gaining ground. Anxieties abound about identity and belonging, loss of community and control – the very things that helped guide the UK to the exit. Even in the Netherlands, one of the most liberal nations in Europe, Geert Wilders, a far-right politician, participates in the governing coalition (when he so chooses).

Protest isn't new. For as long as I can remember, angry farmers have converged in their tractors on the Berlaymont building, depositing manure on the Rue de la Loi. In the 1990s, they were enraged by subsidy cuts linked to agricultural reform. Now it is environmental regulation that stokes revolt. The European Green Deal is controversial – as are national measures to tackle climate change. But leave the merits aside. Focus on the question of who decides. It plainly matters who takes the decision. And it matters who voters *think* takes it.

If an issue is tough or unpopular, national governments often deflect criticism by blaming Brussels. The nature of the system practically invites it: in the Council of Ministers (the EU's main legislative body) national ministers deliberate in private, unobserved by the media or public. Votes are now taken openly but they are rare. Especially with the UK gone, the Commission is usually able to secure compromise without a formal vote. Among insiders, there is plenty of talk and supposition, but a reliable account of who did what and why remains hard to come by. So central Brussels is a reasonable place for the discontented to dump manure.

This peculiar evasiveness allows the EU – and national authorities that defer to it – to engage in horse-trading behind closed doors. It also bypasses the open political negotiation that would allow voters to understand what a law is trying to do. This is arguably not the fault of the EU itself. National governments should inform their own citizens about the questions at stake. Yet on the whole, they don't. This leads the public to mistrust the process.

It doesn't help that the EU seems so creepily conformist, even when it is out on a limb relative to electorates. Geert Mak, veteran Dutch journalist and author of *The Dream of Europe*, points to the Commission as a home of 'true believers' who suffer 'almost physical pain' at criticism of EU policy. 'It's a bubble,' he says, a 'religious sect, complete with its own scripture called the Treaty of the European Union.' Mak is not unsympathetic: as a journalist, he lived in the bubble himself. He has played the game. If you write constructively about the project – explaining and defending it – you will be invited to discussion panels, symposia, keynote speeches. Otherwise, not. That's just how things work in Brussels.

From the EU perspective, it did a good job negotiating the UK's departure and protecting what it saw as its interests. According to proud reminiscences from its chief negotiator, Michel Barnier, the EU blocked the UK from appealing to member states individually. They stuck together and closed ranks to ensure that the Union spoke as one. In this way, they achieved a deal that ensured the mutual economic interests of the UK and member states gave way to the political interests of the EU.

Some years later, campaigning for the French presidency against the EU poster boy Emmanuel Macron, Barnier raised eyebrows by saying that 'people in the bubble of Brussels think they are always right. They don't want to listen. They don't want to change anything. This is precisely the way to provoke more Brexits in Europe.' Running for office in France, he appears to have found a new perspective – or, less generously, a line that he knew would speak to actual voters.

Across Europe – indeed, in much of the developed world – relative economic decline is eroding faith in our political systems. New political parties and leaders suggest that the institutions of liberal democracy don't work, and they are packed with elites who care nothing for the ordinary person. We may not like the messenger, but some of what they say may be true. If we double down on what we are doing, if we refuse to change course and hold the electorate at bay, extremists will act in our place.

Many people here in the UK can hardly bear to think about the referendum and its aftermath. They were fractious, anxious years. People found themselves astounded and angered by others – what are they thinking? What are they doing? But what if – for all the misery and ill-temper, the politicking and chicanery – there was something important going on? Even, perhaps, something good?

Consider it this way: despite profound opposition among much of the political class, the machinery of the British state gave effect to the democratic will of the people, and for the most part it all went through quite peacefully. That this was possible, I suggest, is a testament to the strength of British democracy and its institutions.

The referendum addressed an anxiety about European integration that was real and growing, both within the UK and beyond. As successive new treaties – Maastricht, Amsterdam, Nice, Lisbon – centralised more decision-making power in Brussels, governments recognised that popular consent was needed. In 2005, all three main British parties fought general election campaigns on the promise of a referendum on greater European integration. These promises came to nothing, yet the pressure from sceptics didn't let up. At each election – national and European – the explicitly Euro-sceptic United Kingdom Independence Party increased their share of the vote.

In 2013, the then-prime minister, David Cameron, gave a speech at Bloomberg's HQ in London in which he recognised that 'public disillusion with the EU is at an all-time high'. He continued:

> People feel that the EU is heading in a direction that they never signed up to. They resent the interference in our national life by what they see as unnecessary rules and regulation. And they wonder what the point of it all is. Put simply, many ask 'why can't we just have what we voted to join – a common market?'

He concluded by pledging to renegotiate the UK's relations with the EU, after which the question of future membership would be put to the people in an in/out referendum. Returned to office after the election, the Conservatives put this promise of a referendum into law. In fact, the European Union Referendum Act 2015 passed overwhelmingly, with the support of both major parties.

The following year, on 23 June 2016, the UK voted by 52 per cent to 48 per cent to leave. At 4.39 a.m., David Dimbleby declared 'we are out'. Many will never forget it. Sitting in the BBC studio, Laura Kuenssberg reacted to the news saying, 'it is so rare that as a country and individuals we get the chance to take a decision as big as this. It was the most profound question we had been asked for decades.'

Astonishingly, the electorate had ignored the advice of the establishment and warnings that they would be poorer. As the Vote Leave slogan had put it, 'taking back control' seemed to matter more. It was a true people's revolt.

Inevitably, the establishment's first reaction was to attack those people: they were old and uneducated and came from the north. They should never have been given a say. On the morning of the result, an eminent, previously courteous, barrister approached me and hissed, 'Be in no doubt, we will not let this happen.'

A robust effort was mounted. A caucus (including David Lammy and Keir Starmer) referred to the outcome of the vote as 'catastrophic' and a 'national tragedy', and worked to prevent it being put into effect, believing it would be a historic mistake. Then they proposed a second referendum. Had there been something new to put to the people – a genuinely renegotiated relationship, say – a further vote might have had some justification. But there wasn't.

Parliament, like the country, was divided. Most MPs had backed Remain, while many constituencies voted Leave. Suddenly, it was argued that a referendum was unsuitable to determine such an important and complex issue. That it was 'advisory' only and could be ignored. In this midst of a constitutional upheaval, these tensions could have torn us apart. Twice the Supreme Court was called on to step in, ruling against the government on both occasions. It is worth revisiting these cases – both demonstrate the value of being able to get before a court and how judicial oversight, holding the executive to account, can reassure and keep a system on track.

The first involved a technical point. In October 2016, Theresa May announced that her government would give formal notice of leaving to the EU, as required by Article 50 of the Lisbon Treaty. A Mr Dos Santos brought legal action claiming that Parliament needed to authorise the act. Indeed, he explained that he had voted to leave the EU precisely to preserve parliamentary sovereignty. A banker, Gina Miller, joined (and funded) the litigation with a different motive – to frustrate the leaving process. Other groups joined, too, including Fair Deal for Expats, a sample of the 1.2 million British expats who lived in other EU countries.

The three judges of the Divisional Court ruled in support of the action, and promptly found themselves on the front page of the *Daily Mail*, branded 'Enemies of the People' above photographs of each of them in their wigs – looking, inevitably, 'out of touch' with the people. Liz Truss, then lord chancellor, was slow to condemn personal attacks on the independent judiciary, until a furore mounted, not least from the Bar, and at last she spoke up.

Because of the urgency, the case leapfrogged the Court of Appeal and in January 2017 the Supreme Court heard and dismissed the government's appeal. Parliament passed the necessary legislation and, on 29 March 2017, the PM notified the EU of the intention to exit.

Contrast the handling of another case brought by Fair Deal for Expats, this time before the ECJ. Days after the vote to leave, Commission President Jean-Claude Juncker stated that by 'presidential order' he had forbidden commissioners and director-generals from holding discussions with British representatives. At the time, the UK was still a paying member of the EU. Millions of citizens lived in EU countries other than their own (including in the UK) and sought clarity about their status. Would they be allowed to stay? Would they have to take their children out of school? The ex-pats brought proceedings and the Commission filed a 'confidential' defence, after admitting that Juncker had no power to issue such an order. Even so, the order was extended to member states, and the ECJ declined (without giving reasons) to list an urgent hearing. Instead, it offered a hearing likely to take place a few years in the future. The episode revealed an oppressive improvisation which somehow couldn't be challenged.

In 2019, as the agony of leaving continued, the UK Supreme Court was called on again. It responded promptly and grasped the constitutional nettle. This time it ruled on the legality of the PM Boris Johnson's decision to prorogue Parliament (in effect, to suspend its sitting and conduct of business) for five weeks, until just before the UK was due to leave the EU. The lower court considered this a political judgment that the government was constitutionally permitted to take. The Supreme Court disagreed and ruled the prorogation unlawful.

The case involved (almost) uncharted legal territory. It could, quite probably, have gone either way. Over the centuries, our constitution has evolved. It is not codified in any single authoritative text. In considering the boundary between executive (or 'prerogative') and judicial powers (working out who does what in our system), the Supreme Court drew on precedents that dated back hundreds of years. One of these, the Case of Proclamations, was decided in 'a period of turmoil' when the tussle between Parliament and the Stuart kings led to civil war. The court laid down then that 'the King hath no prerogative, but that which the law of the land allows him'.

In the more recent eighteenth century, when the government was concerned about seditious publications, the courts ruled (in Entick v. Carrington) that state bodies required permission from Parliament (in the form of a statute) to enter and search private property. Relying on these ancient cases, the Supreme Court justified intervening in what it described as a 'one off' situation.

Within days of the judgment, Parliament was back sitting but the stand-off continued. A group of MPs took control of the order paper and legislated to block a no-deal exit, ignoring the government's complaint that this tied its hands in the ongoing negotiations with the EU. Eventually, the opposition agreed to a general election and it was back to the people. The people swung behind the government, delivering the Conservatives their highest share of the popular vote since 1979, and a clear mandate to 'Get Brexit Done'. And that is what happened.

Some were outraged by the Supreme Court's prorogation judgment, condemning it as a judicial power grab. The PM didn't like it, but not complying was never an option. Leaving the EU was a decisive act, by which a deeply controversial vote was put into effect, supervised by an institution that understood the need to determine legality and whose authority was widely accepted. Meanwhile the president of the Supreme Court, Brenda Hale, became a little iconic, not least for the spider brooch she wore while reading the ruling.

If anyone doubts the significance of this, think back to 6 January 2021, when a rioting mob stormed the US Capitol, claiming that the November election had been 'stolen'. Donald Trump refused to accept Joe Biden's victory, declaring to his supporters that 'we will never concede' and goading them to 'resist'.

The entire democratic system relies on loser's consent. After the contest, the losers take their place in the stands. Having flouted this norm, Trump faced impeachment as president. And then, despite strong evidence that in almost any other democracy would have excluded him from holding office again, he was acquitted in a partisan vote in the Senate.

Since returning to the office of the president, Trump has used executive orders to summarily dismiss thousands of federal staff, and to deport and detain supposed illegal immigrants on the slenderest grounds. He has upended the global trading system by imposing punitive tariffs while entirely bypassing Congress.

Even if you like the general cut of his jib, there's a lot that is troubling here. Yuval Levin, an American political analyst, agrees with much of Trump's policy agenda but fears he is undermining the foundations of America's political system. According to the constitutional separation of powers, executive orders (which may turn out to have been illegally used) aren't supposed to bring lasting change; only legislation is meant to do that. So Congress needs to step up and co-operate in a bipartisan way to make deals over concrete things.

It remains to be seen whether Trump's actions are constitutional (unlike EU Commission 'presidential orders', executive orders do exist, although their scope and application are contested). The legal battle will be drawn out. The nightmare scenario, Levin says, is Trump refusing to abide by a ruling. There is good reason to worry; numerous criminal and civil cases have gone against him, to which he has responded by denouncing the proceedings and some of the judges.

The last time I was in DC, I flicked on the TV to hear an interviewee dismiss a court ruling against Trump for being made by a 'Democrat' judge. In the US, many state prosecutors and district attorneys – responsible for deciding whether to bring legal proceedings – are elected. So are many judges. This was once considered a strength; now, in the polarised conditions of current US politics, it leaves them open to accusations of partisanship.

Supreme Court justices are political appointments, as are federal judgeships. This has long been the case and the system has coped. But recently, the appointments and vetting process via the Senate Judiciary Committee have become nakedly partisan. It is an open question whether a ruling of the Supreme Court in the US today would command the authority that allowed the UK to survive its precarious constitutional moment.

On the Continent, too, the tension between legal and political power is present.

In spring 2025, France's National Rally leader, Marine Le Pen, was found guilty of misusing EU funds and banned from office for five years. The ruling, she said, was 'a witch-hunt', and she vowed not to give up her ambition to lead the country. National Rally's president Jordan Bardella called the ruling 'a direct attack on democracy and a wound to millions of patriotic French people'. These are easy slogans to throw about, but many close to the detail say the evidence against Le Pen was strong. However, there may also be truth in the assertion (made by former MEP Daniel Hannan) that the 'flexible and ambiguous' rules are selectively applied. 'Eurosceptics,' he claimed, 'were always investigated more tenaciously, prosecuted more rigorously and penalised more harshly than goody-goody federalists.'

Meanwhile, Romania's constitutional court rejected an application by a defeated presidential candidate, George Simion, described in the British press as 'EU-critical and Trump-admiring', to annul the first-round vote. Simion responded, 'The constitutional court has continued the coup! All we can do is fight! I call you to join me, today and in the coming weeks.'

*

This might get considerably worse, or it might not. All systems come under challenge. To an extent, this unsettling day-to-day struggle is democracy's strength as well as its weakness. These arguments in themselves don't mean the system is broken. Airing and testing different views *is* democracy. Still, to keep our bearings and keep the ship steady, we need some fixed points. Our institutions have to be strong.

Through deliberate reform at the start of the twenty-first century, the UK's Supreme Court emerged from the old House of Lords. It was recognised that some of the old ways were incompatible with modern notions of governance. Judges should no longer be appointed following a 'tap on the shoulder', so a formal, auditable application process was put in its place. And a properly independent judiciary should have no formal link with the legislature, so the Law Lords (as they were called) lost the right to sit in the House of Lords.

The idea of updating an institution to preserve its legitimacy with the public was also visible in the recent coronation ceremony of Charles III. The essentials remained, preserving continuity, but touches like a gospel choir modernised and broadened its appeal.

As a presidential hopeful, Barack Obama recalled that the promise of 'a More Perfect Union' – set out in the preamble to the US Constitution – had launched America's 'improbable experiment called democracy'. The drafters' intent was to create, he said, 'a union which could and should be perfected over time'.

Can the European project also adapt to form a more perfect union, one that can accommodate us in all of our difference? As a nuclear-armed, open economy with clout on the world stage, the UK has a great deal to offer our European friends, as I hope to show in the chapters to come. Previously, the structures and strictures of the EU proved too onerous to command enough public support in the UK. But is there some new, more flexible arrangement that could be put in its place, which doesn't treat the UK as just another third country?

Can the unwieldy EU, with its complex networks of power, interests and influence, update itself? Can it stay true to its roots but adapt? The UK needs a strong partner with whom to meet the challenges of this turbulent time. The EU needs the same from the UK. That is why I am returning to this acrimonious, difficult subject that so alienated colleagues and friends. For me personally, and for the country, Europe is unfinished business. And as old certainties evaporate all around us, there is a historic chance to do better.

Chapter Two

Eurovisions

The EU was created to 'screw' the US, snarls President Trump. The line becomes a regular refrain, justifying tariffs on goods exported by a long-time ally. And yet, when the EU was created back in the 1950s, the US was an enthusiastic sponsor. President Eisenhower put it plainly in his 'Chance for Peace' address, shortly after assuming office in 1953:

> We are ready not only to press forward with the present plans for closer unity of the nations of Western Europe but also, upon that foundation, to strive to foster a broader European community, conducive to the free movement of persons, of trade and of ideas.

As the Iron Curtain descended across Europe, and Communist governments sprang up behind it, America's priority had been to curb Soviet power. Rebuilding the war-shattered economies in the West was one way to do this. So, the US directed millions of dollars in Marshall funds to help Western Europe – including the UK – get back on its feet. As they recovered, these economies also, of course, became important markets for American products.

Lasting peace in Europe was essential to this arrangement. Three times in the last century, France and Germany had fought destructive wars. After Hitler's demise, France wished, in the words of the historian Tony Judt, 'to hold German power down to an unthreatening level', while keeping it productive enough to supply French industry with vital raw materials, such as coal from the Ruhr.

To this end, Jean Monnet, a French federalist and prime architect of the European project, proposed placing the administration of coal and steel, not in the control of any individual state, but rather under a 'supranational' authority to be called the European Coal and Steel Community (ECSC). It was clear that West Germany would only be allowed to rebuild its economy and rejoin the European family if its hands were tied in this way. The West German chancellor, leading a defeated, demoralised and divided country, embraced the trade-off.

The ECSC became the kernel of a wider federalist vision. It was set out in May 1950 in the form of the Schuman Plan, named after the French foreign minister. This novel and ambitious blueprint for the European Economic Community served, in Judt's words, as 'a sort of de facto peace treaty between France and West Germany'. In 1957, the six founder members – France, West Germany, Italy, Belgium, the Netherlands and Luxembourg (the Benelux) – signed the Treaty of Rome establishing the

EEC (which became the EU) and resolving to create 'an ever-closer union among the peoples of Europe'. In integrating their economies, the six were said to be making war between their nations both 'unthinkable' and 'materially impossible'. For the smaller countries, the supranational element (whereby decisions were taken in common bodies, belonging to no single state) was seen as protection against larger, more dominant states.

Britain supported Continental integration, but as a well-wisher, not an active participant. This is often dismissed as 'exceptionalism', but at the time Britain's position *was* different. It was still a global power. The British Empire was crumbling but its former possessions, now independent states, had formed the Commonwealth, with which Britain retained close ties. And crucially, though impoverished by the conflict, Britain avoided occupation and its institutions survived intact. The states of the Third Reich and Vichy France were tainted and swept away: a new German constitution – the *Grundgesetz* – came into being, and in France the Fourth and then Fifth Republics began afresh. By contrast, the sovereignty of Parliament, rooted in a thousand years of history and unaltered by the war, remained central to Britain's political identity. Federalism – in the sense of handing decision-making to a supranational body – would be like fixing something that not only wasn't broken, but which had been refined over centuries of incremental progress and was now rooted deep within the nation's conception of itself.

Still, Britain clearly had to play a part in building the new order. With the US, it helped build global financial institutions like the World Bank and the International Monetary Fund. In Europe, its contribution lay in its sponsorship of two organisations in particular: NATO, the North Atlantic Treaty Organisation, which secured US commitment to Europe's defence; and the Council of Europe, a body dedicated to democracy, human rights and the rule of law. Under the aegis of the Council of Europe, Britain's diplomats and lawyers drafted the European Convention on Human Rights (ECHR), supervised then and now by the European Court of Human Rights in Strasbourg. Nowadays, Conservative politicians criticise decisions of the Strasbourg court, but the Council of Europe generally works in a way that reflects Britain's historic preference for inter-governmental co-operation over federal structures. This preference also led the UK, with six other European countries, to form the European Free Trade Association (EFTA) in January 1960 – a vehicle for economic collaboration without the supranational element.

By 1961, however, with confidence low and the economy flat, the UK changed its mind and decided to apply to join the EU. Twice its approach was blocked by President de Gaulle. In the EU, the UK would be a Trojan horse for the US, De Gaulle declared, because for Britain the US always came first. As De Gaulle's biographer, Julian Jackson, puts it, 'in the long history he carried in his head, England was France's hereditary enemy and historic rival'. Prickliness over perceived slights during the war added to De Gaulle's opposition. Moreover, as he saw it, Britain had the Commonwealth, and France would have Europe.

By the time Britain was let in (over De Gaulle's dead body), the terms on offer were poor. The EU had been moulded to French interests. The Common Agricultural Policy brought industrial Britain no real benefit while ensuring that its contribution to the budget was high. Entry meant joining the customs union, an innately protectionist construct, which damaged trade – and relations – with Australia and New Zealand. The Labour leader, Harold Wilson, had personal ties to New Zealand, and caustically denounced selling 'our friends and kinsmen down the river for a problematic and marginal advantage in selling washing machines in Dusseldorf'. Labour MPs were whipped to oppose joining but large numbers rebelled.

Among those rebels was David Owen MP. Talking to Owen in his home by London's Docklands some fifty years on, I am reminded how starkly Britain's main political parties shifted their positions on Europe. And I am struck by the arc of Owen's career and beliefs. Labour foreign secretary, then leader of the breakaway Social Democratic Party. A one-time enthusiast for the European project who defied his party to join, but who later turned sceptic and ultimately voted to leave. 'We joined it as a common market,' he explained in 2016, 'and more and more it became not a common market but a political union.'

When Labour came to power in 1974, it conducted a performative 'renegotiation' of the deal, then the following year held a referendum on membership, as promised in its manifesto. As PM, Harold Wilson tried to stay above the fray, unlike David Cameron in the more recent referendum. But in fact, there was no real contest. Britain had only been in for two years; the Cold War, in a heavily militarised Europe, created a sense that it was best to stick together. With resignation rather than enthusiasm, the public voted 'In', and without obvious enthusiasm it remained. As Stephen Wall, former British diplomat, who spent five years as the UK's Permanent Representative to the EU, and author of *Reluctant European*, observes, 'Had Britain, like all other member states, enjoyed at least a few early years with clear financial and economic gains from membership, public and parliamentary opinion might have warmed to the project. But it did not.'

Even so, given how much *wasn't* said about Community membership, the apathy of the public is striking. In 1972, Edward Heath's Tory government had quietly signed up to economic and monetary union. Wilson's Labour government rubber-stamped it. Yet during the 1975 referendum campaign, the matter was barely mentioned. As for the question of sovereignty, 'so far, it hasn't been faced,' my father reported from Brussels at the time. 'The fact is that most continental members of the community have committed themselves to a gradual if limited transfer of sovereignty to a still undefined

European power, and they see all community progress as movement in that direction.'

When asked about this, the government said – not incorrectly – that Parliament retained the right to repeal the arrangements for joining. But it did not explain what Wall calls 'the more fundamental point' – that laws passed at EU level could not be changed by a national parliament. The government also omitted to say that the European Court of Justice – a court based in Luxembourg, not London – had the final word on their implementation. In short, the account politicians gave was, in Wall's words, 'more an expression of hope for the kind of Community that Britain would find congenial than an accurate rendering of the reality'.

The reality was more federalist than the British electorate ever appreciated. In the 1975 referendum, there was no substantive discussion of sovereignty, the supremacy of EU law, economic and monetary union, or the European project's core commitment to create an ever-closer union. This mismatch between reality and what the politicians sold to the country – a mismatch that in today's less deferential political climate we'd call a lie – created a deep tension.

Over time, that tension would only grow.

When I found myself back in Brussels fifteen years later, the chatter of keen young Spaniards filled the lecture hall at the Institute of European Studies. We were all excited, I recall, to be part of this venture, to reinvigorate and rebuild Europe through the medium of EU law.

In those days, the EU had policies for agriculture and fish, but no formal 'competence' in environment, energy, telecoms or many of the other areas it deals with today. At the core of the project – then and now – were 'four freedoms': the free movement of goods, persons, services and capital, supported by policies on competition and state aid. Together, these four freedoms were intended to define a common market, later called the internal market, and now the single market.

The Commission was the motor of the project. From its home in the Berlaymont building, a growing posse of politically appointed commissioners proposed legislation – mainly directives (that is, binding targets) and regulations (firm rules) – that would then be haggled over, amended and ultimately signed off by the Council of Ministers, a body made up of government ministers from the member states.

The European Parliament, which sat alternately in Brussels and Strasbourg, was intended to provide a direct link with the citizens of Europe. Its members, elected to the Parliament by voters in each member state, also had a say on legislation, but in those days it was a small one – they were consulted. Now, after a succession of treaty changes, they are joint decision-makers with the Council of Ministers on most important matters.

For us young lawyers, however, the unsung heroes were found in a city 200 kilometres to the south. There, in Luxembourg, the European Court of Justice sat.

The ECJ doesn't get many lines in the Treaty. But,

by the time we were boning up on it in 1989/90, it had established itself as a key driver of European integration. Radical ruling number one established 'direct effect': this gave legal force to directives in each member state, even though the national government in question may not have taken the steps required domestically to put them into law. The Treaty drafters didn't intend directives to work in this way, but the judges reached their decision on policy grounds, not legal ones. The intention, they said, was to give these measures *'effet utile'* – that is, greater practical effect.

Of even greater consequence was the ECJ ruling that EU law overrode conflicting national law. EU law was 'supreme' and took precedence over any legislation at the member-state level. Although the Treaties didn't say this, it was, the court ruled, what the signatories had 'implicitly' agreed.

Our EU law master's degree was taught in French. I wonder if that's why, as I laboured over my Collins dictionary, I failed to notice then how significant these ideas were. Of course I was young, too, and knew nothing about how governments work, about legitimacy or the importance of checks and balances. At the time, I cheered on anything that seemed to strengthen the benevolent and exciting EU legal order.

English law students learn about the law of negligence from a famous case involving a decomposing snail in a bottle of ginger beer. The seminal EU legal dispute was about a more refined drink: the French blackcurrant liqueur Cassis de Dijon.

German law required fruit liqueurs sold in Germany to have a minimum alcohol content of 25 per cent. Cassis had 15 per cent and so could not be exported to Germany. Though their motive was plainly protectionist, the Germans tried to justify the measure on health grounds, arguing that a *lower* alcohol content created *greater* dependency. The ECJ wasn't impressed and struck down the 25 per cent requirement as a breach of the treaty commitment to the free movement of goods. Here, the judges developed the principle of 'mutual recognition': that a product lawfully produced and marketed in one member state should be free to be marketed in any other.

This sweeping approach to deregulation appealed to Prime Minister Thatcher. She joined forces with the British commissioner, Lord Cockfield, and president of the Commission, Jacques Delors, to finally do away with all such non-tariff barriers to trade within Europe. The notional deadline for 'completing' the single market in this way was 1992. Smoothing their path, the Single European Act introduced a kind of legislative 'easy mode' in the Council of Ministers: qualified majority voting. Under QMV, votes were weighted so that support from a percentage of member states (now 55%, representing 65% of the EU population) might suffice to pass laws binding them all. Suddenly, the power of veto became a lot harder to exercise.

But despite the celebrated principle of mutual

recognition and Cassis de Dijon, the Commission always favoured harmonisation – establishing a single agreed Community standard, rather than compelling countries to recognise and respect each others' ways of regulating. Over time, this compulsion to harmonise – and the time and energy taken to achieve it, notwithstanding QMV – became a serious bone of contention.

While I studied, and then practised, EU law, Boris was reporting for the *Daily Telegraph* in Brussels. He filed a multitude of articles, many of which riled both his journalist colleagues and the Commission. A regular theme was the 'threat' posed by harmonised standards to British products and foods or to familiar ways of doing things. 'EC hand reaches out to the grave,' he said of a proposal for a harmonised coffin, which apparently never saw the light of day.

Often the dispute was about additives, such as the red dye, erythrosine, which coloured cocktail cherries and kept British sausages pink. A proposed ban on artificial sweeteners in crisps raised fears that the prawn cocktail flavour might be removed from the market. Other disputes turned on what a product was called. Countries that made chocolate using 100 per cent cocoa products fought for exclusive use of the name. According to Catherine Barnard, Professor of EU Law at the University of Cambridge and author of *The Substantive Law of the EU*, these countries suggested that nations like Britain, Ireland and Denmark, which added vegetable fat, should call their product 'chocolate substitute'. Negotiation and compromise produced a harmonised EU standard for chocolate in the end, but it took twenty-seven years. And that was just over one product.

Many in Brussels thought Boris's stories overblown. At the time I agreed and rolled my eyes with the others. Yet for all that the examples seem vaguely ridiculous, they reflect a deep, near theological conflict: on the one side, diversity and national autonomy; and on the other, a uniformity and central control in the name of 'free movement'. Given the time, cost and restriction often involved in reaching a uniform standard, the question arises, is it worth it? How much does it matter?

The answer will depend on who you are. Businesses wanting to export into multiple markets will probably think it matters a lot. For them, common EU standards (in theory) create certainty. But many people are attached to their prawn cocktail crisps. They like bread-filled, pink (when raw) sausages even if Continentals think them disgusting. And if it isn't a health risk, why interfere? There is a lot of emotion around food.

Nowadays the Cassis de Dijon case wouldn't arise: there is a harmonised EU standard on alcohol content, so EU rules govern the matter exclusively.

Delors and Mrs Thatcher agreed about the single market, but they fell out over federalism. Delors was a French socialist, an avowed federalist and a passionate supporter of economic and monetary union. In 1988, Mrs Thatcher gave a now-famous speech outlining her contrasting vision of Europe. Stephen Wall (who served three prime ministers) wrote the first draft. When he reread it with Tony Blair years later, the two men agreed that it contained nothing very extreme. And yet, against the integrationist orthodoxies of the late eighties, it sounded like heresy.

First, the prime minister spoke out strongly for decentralisation. She said she wanted Europe to work more closely 'on the things we can do better together than alone'. But, she said, this did not 'require power to be centralised in Brussels or decisions to be taken by an appointed bureaucracy'. 'Indeed,' she continued, 'it is ironic that just when . . . the Soviet Union . . . [is] learning that success depends on dispersing power and decisions away from the centre, there are some in the Community who seem to want to move in the opposite direction.'

Mrs Thatcher's vision of Europe as a 'family of nations' was in direct conflict with Delors's desire for a supranational federation. He wanted, he said, the European Parliament to be the democratic body of the Community, the Commission its executive and the Council of Ministers its senate. 'No, no, no,' was Mrs Thatcher's emphatic response in the House of Commons. (The next day, the *Sun*'s headline, 'Up Yours Delors', affirmed its agreement.)

For as long as she could, Thatcher resisted joining the Exchange Rate Mechanism (ERM), a scheme in which different national currencies were loosely pegged to one another, limiting their relative fluctuations. In the end, however, the clamour was too great, and she gave in. With her support ebbing away, she stepped down in November 1990.

John Major took over. After a surprise election win, he agreed a new treaty on European integration. Signed at Maastricht in the Netherlands, it granted the EU new areas of competence and paved the way for a single European currency.

One night soon after, I awoke in my flat on the Avenue Molière in Ixelles to find the building shaking. Above the mantlepiece, a large gilt frame had shifted and hung precariously. I learnt the next morning that it was an earthquake – its epicentre in Maastricht. The political sketches wrote themselves.

Any predictions of doom appeared to have been fulfilled a couple of months later, when 50.7 per cent of voters in Denmark rejected the Treaty of Maastricht after a high turnout. In the UK, Major similarly struggled to get the treaty ratified, given his narrow parliamentary majority and a loud clutch of rebels he dubbed 'the bastards'. He managed it in the end, but only at the cost of several confidence votes.

In Brussels, meanwhile, Boris and I had become close. One autumn, at what seemed an intimate moment, he mused: 'Who'd have thought?'

'Who'd have thought what?' I asked, expecting something like, 'You and me, after all these years . . .'

'That sterling would crash out of the ERM.'

Black Wednesday, 16 September 1992. Inside the Exchange Rate Mechanism, sterling was under pressure. German interest rates were high when the UK needed them to be low. The government spent billions trying to prop up the currency, but there was a massive run on the pound. By 7 p.m. Britain gave up the fight. At the next election, the Tories were toast.

Neither the Danish vote, nor Britain's travails, halted the move towards greater European integration. Joyful to be free from Soviet control, the newly independent countries of wider Europe exuded a hunger to emulate the West. We Euro-lawyers, mostly in our twenties and early thirties, travelled East to share our 'expertise'. Brimming with confidence and optimism, I addressed conferences in Ljubljana and Budapest on EU environment and energy policy, unconcerned that I knew nothing about the places where I was speaking. The past was of no consequence; only the future mattered – and, helpfully, it was already mapped out in the Community *acquis* (settled rules). These countries had only to adopt them without demur.

In a similar spirit of excitement, demand was building for the reunification of East and West Germany. This, in turn, created an unstoppable impetus behind the adoption of a new single currency. Beneath the stirring, universalist mood music, the deal was in essence a bilateral transaction: the French would accept reunification only if Germany agreed to the euro, binding it tightly into European structures, which France hoped would give it leverage over the German economy.

Tony Blair, a three-term (almost) prime minister, never took Britain into the euro. His chancellor, Gordon Brown, devised five economic tests to determine whether to do so. It is unclear whether Brown opposed joining on principle, but the time wasn't right, he pronounced repeatedly. Labour did, however, significantly increase Brussels' reach into national law, opting into the Social Chapter, a new EU competence on workers' rights. For many Labour politicians and supporters, this stoked a new enthusiasm for the European project.

On the Conservative side, it fed a growing grievance. Major's government chose to stay out of the Social Chapter (agreed at Maastricht). In order to get around this and ensure all member states were bound – ignoring the UK's objections – the EU used its competence in health and safety matters to adopt the Working Time Directive (urged on by France). This fixed minimum working hours and holiday entitlements. The ECJ predictably rejected the UK's legal challenge. Another feature of the EU system is the 'one-way' ratchet: a law passed at EU level can only be changed at EU level, and doing so is usually a lengthy and laborious process. Once given away, a competence can't be unilaterally reclaimed. Because these workers' rights were adopted at EU level, they therefore became entrenched, which pleased Labour as much as it displeased the Conservatives.

Further integration meant further Treaty change and, in some member states, the people were consulted. But when asked their view, again many people didn't like what was on offer. In 2005, in referenda held in France and the Netherlands – founding members of the EU – voters comprehensively rejected the Constitutional Treaty, which its leaders had agreed. Soon after, Blair gave a soul-searching, oddly prescient speech to the European Parliament:

> I have sat through council conclusions after council conclusions describing how we are 'reconnecting Europe to the people'. Are we? It is time to give ourselves a reality check . . . The people are blowing trumpets round the city walls. Are we listening? Have we the political will to go out and meet them so that they regard our leadership as part of the solution not the problem?

The answer, sadly, was no: the Constitutional Treaty was repackaged as the Lisbon Treaty and passed without further consulting the people.

Now that the machinery was in place, the 2008 financial crash tested it to breaking point. At first, we were fixated on Wall Street: Lehman Brothers going bust, traders filing onto the street with potted plants crammed into boxes. The following year, however, the effects started to show in the eurozone.

In Greece it was especially grim. The government was broke and unable to service its huge debts. Having joined the euro, there was no option of devaluing its currency to boost exports and lower borrowing costs. The combined European Central Bank (ECB), Commission and the IMF, known as the Troika, arranged a series of bailouts, but the price they demanded – stringent austerity measures – shrunk the Greek economy by a quarter. Twenty-five thousand public servants were laid off, and as prices shot up, poverty rose.

Desperation bred violence and disorder. Why, people wondered, was Greece in the euro in the first place? Surely – as a country heavily in debt – it did not meet the convergence criteria set out in Maastricht. Indeed not, but as a strategic gateway to Asia, and as the birthplace of democracy, Greece had to be in. This was, after all, a political project.

Yanis Varoufakis, Greece's finance minister during these years, is scathing about the medicine that the Troika imposed on his country. Austerity compounded the suffering, he says, and democracy was treated with contempt. Among Greeks, the German-led ECB was especially resented, its edicts compared by some to the Nazi occupation. Protesters compared Angela Merkel to Adolf Hitler. As politicians called for debt relief from Germany, others demanded compensation for Nazi atrocities during the war.

Clearly, the rush to construct a single currency – the long-nurtured dream of federalists – was not promoting peace. Quite the opposite.

During the British military deployment in Afghanistan, I was part of a team defending claims against the government brought under the Human Rights Act (HRA) and European Convention on Human Rights. The law was in flux, making these difficult cases. Some recent decisions from the human rights court in Strasbourg had extended its jurisdiction. With troops losing their lives, a right-of-centre think tank began to argue that the HRA was, in effect, forcing them to fight with their arms tied behind their backs.

In the year leading up to the 2016 referendum, I was surprised to find claimants relying on yet another European rights instrument, the EU's Charter of Fundamental Rights. In some cases it merely duplicated settled ECHR rights, but in others it invoked vaguely worded new ones such as the 'right to good administration'. Where did this come from, I wondered? Hadn't the UK opted out of it?

When the Charter appeared as part of the Lisbon Treaty, Tony Blair's government had indeed opposed it. With Poland, they negotiated an opt-out, contained in Protocol 30. When the Charter was discussed in the Commons, on 27 June 2007, Blair assured the House, 'it is absolutely clear that we have an opt-out.'

This was repeated by other ministers. Questioned in the Commons about the Charter in 2011, Ken Clarke, the Conservative lord chancellor, said he doubted that the ECJ would challenge pre-existing EU law by reference to the Charter since doing so would 'defy' the Charter as well as Protocol 30. But Ken's confidence was misplaced. The ECJ did precisely what he had assured Parliament it would not do. In a case about privacy and 'digital rights', it struck down a directive, ignoring its own previous judgment and rendering invalid national security laws in five member states, including the UK.

The ECJ also ruled that the Charter applied in the UK (and Poland) in the same way as in other member states. Protocol 30, it said, was a 'political' text, without legal effect. So, despite what the PM told Parliament, there was no opt-out.

I was enraged. I'll try to explain why.

1. Two member states made clear their opposition to the Charter. This was accepted by the other member states and put into writing. But the ECJ didn't accept it. The question therefore arose: who is in charge? The court or the member states?

2. If the ECJ was in charge and an opt-out wasn't enough, how could a member state ever resist further integration? How can you say no and be sure this is respected?

3. The Charter mattered because EU law is supreme. It overrides any national law with which it conflicts, including any Act of Parliament or constitutional amendment. Any national measure found in breach of the Charter can be set aside (which is why claimant lawyers wanted to use it). This gives the ECJ enormous power.

4. Also, the Charter was a poorly drafted measure that would create confusion, duplication and uncertainty. The Charter was said to reflect existing law, yet it

contained fifty rights to the ECHR's twenty or so. If a national court was uncertain about the scope of a right, it was obliged to refer the matter to the ECJ for a definitive answer. This would create delay and give further scope to the court to extend both its own jurisdiction and the reach of the Charter. Those seeking to downplay the significance of the Charter argued that it only applied when *EU law* was being implemented. But the problem was – for goodness sake – that nobody had any idea what was national and what was EU law. When analysts tried to work out how much UK law actually came from the EU during the 2016 referendum, they settled on a range of *6 to 84 per cent*. I know this is a rant. But finally, I thought it was hard enough to maintain public support for the ECHR, despite its noble pedigree. This dog's dinner would undermine the whole edifice of human rights law. In my despair, I concluded it was a Charter of Profound Incoherence.

In light of all this, I marvelled at how frequently the Home Secretary, Theresa May, complained about the ECHR and HRA. They were tame! When Parliament enacted the HRA, it took care to respect parliamentary sovereignty. Under the HRA, a court can't strike down an Act of Parliament: in the event of a breach, the most it can do is formally invite the government to bring forward legislation to remedy it. This alone was enough to drive Theresa May mad. Yet when the ECJ extended its reach with the Charter, drastically reducing the scope for decisions at national level, we looked away. Why was that?

There were two reasons, I think. First, governments tend to worry about immediate things, things people think about when they go out to vote. Here in the UK, the Charter hadn't yet come to many people's attention, which meant it was a problem for tomorrow, not today. Second, governments want to be considered good Europeans, not table-thumpers or handbag wielders like Mrs Thatcher. Of course it's good to co-operate, even conciliate, but there are limits.

This was mine. I tried to unthink it, but once the worries set in, they only multiplied.

Here's an example of the kind of thing I found myself brooding on. In the Lisbon Treaty, the member states agreed that the EU should itself sign up to the European Convention on Human Rights, which would mean that the Strasbourg court could rule on the legality of the acts of EU institutions. This would be good for the rule of law in the EU. It would mean, for example, proper accountability for bodies such as Frontex, the EU's border control agency, which an internal investigation in 2022 found to be responsible for systematic human rights violations on the external border.

Yet the ECJ, sitting in Luxembourg, has said no, claiming that the EU signing up to the ECHR would undermine the 'Community legal order'. This is widely understood as a turf war. Professor Philippe Sands has described the ECJ's position as 'an expression of self-interest intended to maintain a degree of judicial monopoly'. In other words, the ECJ in Luxembourg doesn't want to be subject to another judicial body. If it can fend off Strasbourg, it avoids outside scrutiny. So there the judges sit, at the summit of the European political edifice, an anonymous professional clique, protecting a legal order they constructed themselves, seemingly impervious to direction from the elected leaders of member states.

In 2024, at the Council of Europe in Strasbourg, I was told that an announcement about the EU finally acceding to the ECHR was due any day. Eighteen years on from the Lisbon Treaty commitment, it hasn't happened yet. Having defied the member states for so long, I now doubt it ever will.

In 2016, looking at the wider canvas, we were, as I saw it, giving up our decision-making powers bit by bit, without accountability, visibility or control. Lawyer friends often agreed there was a serious problem with the EU legal order. Academic journals criticised poorly reasoned cases. Yet these issues stayed well below the radar of public opinion. Even by the time of the referendum, there was no real move for legal reform.

There were other things, too. It felt like Britain's influence in the EU was ebbing away. Outside the eurozone, we were no longer a key player. And on laws that mattered to Britain, such as the regulation of banks, we were being outvoted in the Council of Ministers.

Even over something as important as the appointment of Commission president, Cameron was sidelined. Jean-Claude Juncker, a dour old-school federalist from Luxembourg, rumoured to take long liquid lunches, was not an inspiring choice. Cameron understood that Angela Merkel, among others, shared this view. At the last minute though, Merkel succumbed to domestic political pressure to follow the *Spitzenkandidaten* system. This was a 'procedure' conjured up by the European Parliament whereby the 'lead candidate' of the largest party in the Parliament would become Commission president. The mechanism was wholly unknown in Britain, and the Council subsequently disputed its legality. It was shelved in 2019, when Ursula von der Leyen became president. Ignoring the view of a large, net-contributing member state like the UK was insulting and counterproductive given anxieties in the UK about diminishing influence and the project's direction. But on top of that, the pantomime process, in which ambush took the place of negotiation, was exasperating.

On 3 February 2016, Cameron presented to the Commons the 'renegotiation' promised in 2013 – a device designed to smooth the way to a yes vote. The UK, he announced, would no longer be held to the Treaty aim of 'ever-closer union'. We could resist further political integration. On the face of it, this hardly seemed like a victory: we had already chosen to stay out of big projects like the euro and the Schengen free-movement area. We had opted out of most justice and home affairs measures. What was the gain here?

The real issue with 'ever-closer union' concerned the European Court of Justice.

The ECJ interprets EU law 'purposively' to align with the aims of the Treaties. This means that the aim to create an ever-closer union is baked into most of what the court does. The text Cameron presented stated that 'ever-closer union' shouldn't be used to 'support an extensive interpretation' of EU powers or to extend the scope of legislation. But the court sees this as its role. Why would it change to placate a single recalcitrant member state? Given the fate of the UK's Charter opt-out, I thought it almost certain that Cameron's new assurances would be ignored, too.

Under the heading of benefits and free movement, the Cameron deal said that, when deciding whether a person seeking entry to the UK posed a threat to 'public policy or security', national authorities 'may take into account past conduct of the individual concerned and the threat may not always need to be imminent'. This provision reversed a previous ECJ judgment.

Most people, I am sure, never appreciated that the ECJ used to lay down rules as detailed as this on issues like entry clearance. Controlling borders is a core function of government. It seemed utterly wild to me that a major diplomatic initiative, involving heads of state meeting over the course of six months, was needed to get *permission* to act to keep UK citizens safe.

Another core function of government is deciding how to allocate taxpayers' money through the benefits system – another area where specific permissions were sought (and granted to only a limited extent). In any event, Cameron's deal would not eliminate this kind of intrusive micro decision-making. It would address a few pressing issues that he had selected, but the system as a whole would remain as it was, with decisions that were rightly the purview of national governments (accountable to the electorate) being taken by the EU.

Another oddity in the deal was its declaration that national security was a matter for the member states to decide for themselves. The Treaty was already crystal clear on this point, so why did it need to spell that out? Well, because again and again, EU institutions found ways around the Treaty, justifying their intervention in terms of free movement, privacy or data protection as the occasion suggested. As for the Charter, Cameron's deal repeated the wording of Protocol 30 (believed by Blair to be an opt out). But given the Protocol had already been ruled ineffective, this looked like a waste of ink.

It seemed to me that no meaningful reform would take ever place. We would vote to stay, and then this unambitious fudge of an agreement would unravel or wither. By that point, the impetus for EU reform would have gone. With the problems unaddressed and our self-respect as a self-governing nation further reduced, it would be even harder to walk away. Choosing that option didn't seem right. Tempting as it was, I saw it as betraying the next generation for the sake of a quiet life.

I didn't see the dividing lines as the UK v. the EU. I

had no animus towards Cameron or Osborne, who were always charming (at least to my face). But the renegotiation and referendum felt like short-term political tactics when our long-term national interest was at stake. I feared it was all spin, secret plans and clever tricks. I was angry with the whole political class.

That didn't make the choice any easier.

What I did in the privacy of the polling booth, no one would know or very much care. For Boris, the stakes were higher.

Boris was lobbied from all directions. He knew that I had always supported the European project and now had serious doubts. Our families, on the other hand, were strongly in favour of staying.

He was struggling to decide his position. I suggested, as he prepared to write his weekly *Telegraph* column, that he should set out two arguments – one for Leave, the other Remain. See how that comes out, I said. As it turned out, someone told the press about these two opposing versions of his article, and this has – unfairly, I think – been taken to reveal opportunism and a lack of conviction. To me it was natural to test the strength of a case by writing it down. I'd always found it helped clear my head.

After the referendum was called and Boris had declared his position, I met Gisela Stuart, the Labour MP for Birmingham Edgbaston and chair of Vote Leave. Appointed by Blair to work on the (ultimately discarded)

EU Constitutional Treaty, she was turned by that experience, concluding that the EU as a construct had no real motivation to become accountable to the people. Gisela was German. I was born in West Berlin (and my father in Bremen, in northwest Germany). At the time I met Gisela, those supporting Leave were being painted as insular little Englanders. I knew I wasn't one, but still felt out on a limb for worrying about where we were headed. I found Gisela's outlook immensely reassuring.

I never saw the now-notorious campaign bus, but Gisela travelled on it with Boris. 'We send the EU £350 million per week. Let's fund our NHS instead'. The slogan seemed a bit crude at the time, and I thought it unwise to quote a gross figure for the UK's contribution. Now, when relatively small slices to public expenditure create such heated debate, I see it a bit differently. I think it was legitimate to point out how much we were paying to be in the EU. It was fair enough to ask whether the money might be better spent on other things.

From the days of Mrs Thatcher demanding our money back, the outsized UK contribution had been a thorny topic. Until the bus came around, the public had no idea what the cost of membership was. In 2016, dispute over the net figure provoked extensive discussion, including the degree to which the UK could choose how any money that came back would be spent. Gross or net, these were huge sums.

The other highly contentious issue during the referendum campaign turned out to be immigration, which two groups in particular seemed to play up. The first was UKIP and Leave.eu (not the official campaign for Leave). They, most infamously, produced a callous and misleading poster of Syrian refugees on the Slovenia–Croatia border, captioned 'Breaking Point: The EU has failed us all'. The other was the Remain campaign, which clearly preferred accusing Leave supporters of racism to actually discussing the merits of the EU. The UKIP poster made that deflective manoeuvre much easier for them.

Although its campaign slogan covered taking back control of money, laws and borders, the Vote Leave campaign didn't push the issue of immigration. It simply noted that membership meant millions of EU nationals had a legal right to relocate to Britain, so Cameron's pledge to reduce immigration to the tens of thousands was impossible to fulfil. That signalled two things: one, a lack of honesty with the electorate; and, two, an absence of control on an issue many people cared deeply about.

The level of immigration was not a significant worry for me, but I recognised its salience to the question of who makes the rules; in other words, sovereignty. By 2016, the right to free movement had been extended, bit by bit, well beyond the original focus on workers, to those *looking for* work. This had come about through legislation and expansive interpretation by the ECJ. 'EU citizenship' was introduced by the Treaty of Maastricht, which shifted a whole host of decisions about borders and benefits away from member states.

I didn't campaign, but I went to the TV debates. The

Remain teams never presented a rousing case for the EU. The message seemed to be 'you will be poorer; racists support Leave; and Boris is a cad'. That last bit may have been true but it wasn't the point.

The unedifying was soon pursued by the unprintable. A few weeks into the race, a story went around that a new female QC, married to a senior Conservative, had had a drunken romp outside Waterloo Station, and that this QC was me. At first, I wasn't especially bothered; on the day in question I was out of the country with my family, as could easily have been verified. Our children thought the whole thing was very funny, a detail about knickers especially. Yet as the rumours intensified I felt people avoiding me.

A barrister friend traced the source of the story to a domain in Ireland, but there the trail went cold and I gave up hope of vindication. Finally, to my surprise, the *Sun* broke the story as an example of Remain dirty tricks. Lynton Crosby told me later he had confronted Cameron about the slurs ('Below the belt, mate', I imagine him saying). Cameron apparently brushed him off, saying 'well, they got personal about me'. I am not suggesting Cameron was directly involved. Grubby business, though, politics.

The morning of the result, David Cameron resigned. He had promised he wouldn't, but he did, leaving the country rudderless at a critical time. Gathered around the TV at home, the mood was sombre.

Weeks vanished into a leadership contest. We were

leaving the house for Boris's campaign launch when phones buzzed with the news that his campaign ally Michael Gove had jumped ship and launched his own bid. Later that day I was back at the house alone when Dominic Cummings turned up on the doorstep, in tears. I told him I had no idea why Gove did what he did. We spoke for a while but I was guarded, suspecting that he knew more than I. None of them seemed all that trustworthy to me. So, failing to muster much sympathy for Dom in his distress, I sent him on his way.

Though I was ostensibly still working, my role as the foreign secretary's wife meant I spent a good deal of time having lunch. In that emotional period, I lunched with the EU ambassadors' spouses, in part to get across that the vote didn't mean we disliked Europe or Europeans. We met at Carlton Gardens, the foreign secretary's official residence, and the Polish Hearth Club in South Kensington. We were, it was understood, expressing our personal views. Someone spoke about the 'beauty' of EU decision-making, how different countries negotiated, compromised and reached agreement.

I have thought a lot about this since. I understand what she meant, but I don't share that view. Whichever way I turn the thing, for me it always comes down to this: even if people are not actually watching what happens in the parliament chamber, even if lots of detailed work happens in committees where hardly any members of the public bother to venture, the debate about our laws needs to be visible. And we need to be able to change them – fast – if they turn out to be bad or if circumstances change.

On 29 March 2017, the (Polish) president of the European Council, Donald Tusk, received the UK's Article 50 letter triggering departure. I watched it on the news in Carlton Gardens. I admire the Polish nation and knew Tusk to be an Anglophile. His sadness was plain to see and I shared it.

That evening the British PM, Theresa May, and her husband Philip came for dinner – just the four of us. They brought an amaryllis bulb in an M&S pot. I planted it out and watched it grow impressively into bloom until, all too soon, it was spent and keeled over. Not much later, on 28 July 2018, Mrs May resigned as prime minister, unable to pass her exit deal through the Commons. Having mustered the courage to 'take back control' myself, I'd resigned my spousal role shortly before, for reasons unconnected with politics.

Finally, on Christmas Eve 2019, with Ursula von der Leyen leading the Commission, and my estranged husband leading the UK, a Trade and Cooperation Agreement (TCA) was concluded. It came through against the odds, and was a massive relief. Whatever the EU was meant to be, the thing it had become was something very difficult to escape. For a time, it seemed likely that the democratic vote would be thwarted. And yet, we were out.

Chapter Three

Ever Tighter

We were out, but far from at peace – either among ourselves or with our European neighbours. Discord and ill-feeling, generated by the 2016 vote, seemed to poison so many interactions. When a coronavirus appeared from China, we locked down to try to combat it, shuttering our economies and suspending normal life. I had greater distance from political events, but my preoccupation with the European project persisted. Once we tentatively opened up and travel resumed, I went first to Northern Ireland, where – to my shame – I had never before been.

The IRA's campaign of terror formed a backdrop to my adolescence. Sometimes the bombs managed to kill: the explosion that ripped apart Lord Mountbatten's boat took his life and that of his grandson, among others. Thatcher and her government survived the blast at Brighton's Grand Hotel (though others weren't so lucky). The victims weren't always public figures: ordinary people were also killed, going to work or having a drink in the pub. In London, parents worried when we went shopping, but in Northern Ireland many more people's lives were blighted or destroyed by the Troubles. In 1998, the Good Friday Agreement (GFA) was signed to wide-spread disbelief and delight after many years' negotiation, near collapse of the talks, and a final, historic coming together.

My daughter, Cassia, studied at Trinity College in Dublin, and made good friends from the North. Inserting myself into a visit to one Belfast-based friend, I had a secret agenda: to check out the supermarket shelves, now apparently depleted thanks to the Northern Ireland (NI) Protocol.

The Protocol formed part of the UK's Withdrawal Agreement. The EU's stated aim was to protect the 'integrity' of the single market by ensuring that goods that did not comply with its harmonised standards would not reach the Republic (at that point of course UK products met the same standards). To avoid inflaming sectarian tensions, EU checks on imports could not take place at the border between Northern Ireland and the Republic, it was said. Instead, any checks would take place at points of entry from mainland Britain (GB).

Come early 2021, with the UK a 'third country' as the regime came into effect, a whole range of products were suddenly banned: cold cuts of meat, seed potatoes, apple trees. Pets were denied entry and parcels were blocked. In effect, a new border had appeared in the Irish Sea. The late David Trimble, as leader of the Ulster Unionist Party, co-negotiated the Good Friday Agreement and, at great personal risk, persuaded the Unionist community to support it. In 2021, he warned that the NI Protocol was subverting the 'careful balance' of the Agreement. Ninety per cent of businesses in Northern Ireland didn't sell outside of the province, yet they had to engage in costly and disruptive checks. The EU conducted more checks in Northern Ireland, Trimble pointed out, 'than on all trade coming through the EU's eastern frontier, a known smuggling route, or even Rotterdam, the EU's main entrance for goods from the rest of the world'. It was, Trimble said, treating 'Northern Ireland as a political football'.

By July, the government in Westminster tabled proposals to address the problem – to no avail. You chose Brexit, you signed the agreement. *Voilà.* The government extended grace periods and drafted legislation to suspend the Protocol, a move that was furiously condemned by the EU, member states, the government's opponents and others.

Meanwhile, as the EU struggled to obtain sufficient vaccine supplies, the Commission introduced new controls that required vaccine manufacturers in the EU to get central approval to export. The Commission also triggered Article 16 of the NI Protocol to prevent the movement of vaccines from the Republic to the North, creating (among other things) the very border they claimed was inimical to peace. The Commission quickly backed down, but it confirmed a belief in some quarters that the border issue had been overplayed, 'weaponised', to inflict pain on reprobate Britain.

In February 2023, changes were agreed to mitigate these problems. The Windsor Framework introduced a green lane for goods not destined for the EU but sold in Northern Irish supermarkets and unlikely to cross the border into the Republic. Other sensible measures – such as data sharing, oversight based on risk and intelligence, and the removal of 1,700 pages of EU rules – eased the friction, both social and economic.

The Protocol still evokes strong feelings, and people have very different takes on these events. Some may think my summary is partial. What I take from the row and its (quasi) resolution is that the EU adopts a position of technical impartiality that conceals a hard-edged political choice. Just as it chose to move from maximalist checks to a more proportionate system based on the reality of risk, so it could moderate its stand in other areas if it perceived a gain to itself in doing so. Not being bamboozled by references to the 'rules' is important for the future.

By 2023, the worst of Covid was behind us. My other daughter, Lara, had married Patrick, a young man from Germany, and we took advantage of the loosened travel restrictions to meet up with his parents in the Rhine-land, to taste Riesling and pick grapes at Weingut Trenz, where they had bought us each a sponsored vine.

We were staying in Kaub. In the early morning I went for a wander, and lingered by the imposing statue of *Generalfeldmarschall* Gebhard Leberecht von Blücher. Who was this old Prussian? Someone rather interesting, it turned out, and important. In a small museum round the corner, I learnt that from Kaub he had launched a daring expedition to push back Napoleon, constructing at speed, in the dark, floating platforms over the Rhine.

Later, transported by cable car, we visited the *Niederwalddenkmal*, a colossal monument that looms over the river and the lush valley below. Germania's arm stretches high, to celebrate victory over the French and the unification of Germany in 1871. White panels below explained in German and English that, in glorifying the German Empire, the history we saw here was 'distorted'. I thought back to Judt's description of the founding of the EU, and France's desire to 'hold German power down to an unthreatening level'. The cringing text was certainly consistent with that.

On a separate occasion we met up with Patrick's parents, Hanne and Jürgen, in Leipzig, once an important city of the former East Germany. Field Marshall Blücher, it emerged, had been here too. In fact, he commanded the Prussian army of Silesia, overcoming Napoleon at the Battle of Leipzig. Then he joined forced with Wellington to defeat Napoleon once and for all at the Battle of Waterloo.

Today, though we (and ABBA) refer to these battles fairly often, the Germans don't. They did during the Third Reich, however. In fact, they honoured the Prussian victory in concrete and granite, building the *Völkerschlachtdenkmal*, Monument to the Battle of the Nations. We climbed its 500 steps, awestruck and a little horrified at the size of the thing. Isn't there some happy medium, I wondered, between self-flagellating confessions of distortion and these gargantuan monuments to victory?

After the Nazis were vanquished and the Third Reich was gone, there was understandably a strong desire in Continental Europe to end forever this back-and-forth of war, destruction and displacement. Months after the Berlin Wall fell, my son-in-law was born. As it happened, he had spent six years studying graphic design in Leipzig, and eagerly showed us the city, though he had never been to the *Völkerschlachtdenkmal*. For him, Germany's dark past had no special allure. He is an art director living in London, a grateful beneficiary of peace and, it must be said, the earlier right of free movement of people. At his urging, we visited the Bauhaus in nearby Dessau, a more uplifting German gift to the world.

Modern Germany exemplifies the change that is upsetting the established European order. For my entire adult life, Germany seemed resolutely focused on pursuing prosperity – through European structures – and trading with the world. *Wandel durch handel* (change through trade) was the backbone of its foreign policy, justifying close economic ties with authoritarian regimes. And it worked: until very recently, the German economy was considered *the* success story of Europe. Now, though, geopolitics has intruded and the three elements that sustained its economic miracle have collapsed: reliance on cheap Russian gas; dependence on exports of manufactured goods to China; and low defence spending, made possible by the US security umbrella. For years Angela Merkel was seen as the leading statesperson in Europe, but almost as soon as she left the scene, her legacy unravelled.

In his book, *Kaput, The End of the German Miracle*, Wolfgang Münchau submits these failures to forensic examination. The culprit, he finds, is culture: a closed, mutually dependent relationship between politicians and business, uninterested in geopolitics, focused only on selling the old products in the old way, and in the process becoming technologically backward. 'It worked until it didn't,' he says.

By way of example, Münchau accuses successive German governments of colluding with the car industry and, most damningly, of helping them even after they installed cheating devices to mislead emissions testers. Instead of investing in electric cars or technology (as China did), 'the German car industry went to criminal extremes to keep the old technology kicking for a little while longer'.

'Technophobia,' he writes, 'goes hand in hand with elitism.'

Harsh as this critique sounds, it appears to chime with the experience of Sir James Dyson, the leading British entrepreneur, who battled to break into a market dominated by big German business – protected, he says, by the EU. The EU adopted an energy-use labelling system for vacuum cleaners, to better inform consumers about products on the market and to encourage manufacturers to reduce the energy consumption of their products.

Dyson Ltd, which markets bagless vacuum cleaners, took issue with the test of energy use devised by the Commission, which tested machines while they were empty. The relevant rules stipulated, however, that tests be done in conditions which reflected 'normal' or 'actual' use. Normal or actual use – as the court eventually found – meant with the vacuum cleaner's receptacle partially filled, not empty. Consequently, five years after Dyson first lodged the claim, the Commission's energy labelling regulation was annulled.

The test appears to defy common sense. Washing machines, ovens and dishwashers are not tested empty. So why were vacuum cleaners? The typically sparse ECJ judgment does not explain, but according to Dyson, testing an empty machine benefitted manufacturers of bagged cleaners – which tend to clog in actual use – by overstating their energy efficiency. An international standards organisation, the International Electrotechnical Commission, had adopted a dust-loaded test but, following lobbying by large German manufacturers, the Commission ignored this, choosing to adopt its own empty-machine test instead. According to Dyson, this misled consumers and stifled the use of innovative technology for years. It also caused his company financial loss, for which he is – unsuccessfully so far – seeking damages before the ECJ. Meanwhile, in the ladies' loos in Frankfurt Airport, I discover a kind of justice as Dyson's Airblades blast my hands dry.

From the outset, the European project has enabled Germany to cultivate a 'business first' approach to the world. Through NATO, others took care of defence, leaving Germany to focus on commerce and the interests of specific champion industries. For a long time, no one challenged this; indeed, they encouraged it. Germany's economic success was seen as Europe's gain, while its reticence in military and geopolitical matters was reassuring.

But, just as bagged vacuum cleaners feel out of date, so does the notion that German political power should be suppressed, rather than channelled. Germany is a large country, and what it does affects the rest of the Continent. This calls for care. But for over a decade, the worry about Germany has not been that it acts but that it doesn't. As Radek Sikorski, Poland's foreign minister, observed at the time of the sovereign debt crisis: 'I fear German power less than German inaction.' Coming from a Pole, that was quite something.

For France, sponsoring the euro as a means to constrain Germany didn't pay off. Far from it: the new currency turbo-charged German exports, allowing its economy to flourish, while the French struggled with debt. As Germany got richer, French discontent grew, until it cast a shadow over the euro, the EU and the entire political class.

Many advanced Western economies face similar problems. Traditional industrial jobs have been lost. Birth rates are low and populations are ageing. Welfare is expensive and mass immigration strains social cohesion. Even so, Brigitte Granville, author of *What Ails France?*, sees special pathologies in France's response.

Granville is professor of International Economics at

Queen Mary University. She finds that the 'top-down', technocratic rule imposed on the French republic by its 'oligarchic' political class has fuelled indebtedness and chronically high structural unemployment. So, she says, has 'official France's instinct to impose layers of complex regulation on all kinds of economic activity'.

The same instinct is reflected in Europe's monetary union, which Granville sees as a scheme to 'protect and project French power', though it now threatens European democracy. Despite very muted popular support, the 'political elite' (mainly *énarques*, graduates of the French civil service academy the ENA) was intent on proceeding with the euro, she says. Pressure from the financial markets convinced these technocrats that sovereignty no longer existed, at least in the monetary sphere, and this reinforced the idea of a Europe-wide technical solution. In the September 1992 referendum, the French public voted yes to Maastricht by the narrowest of margins: 51.04 per cent, setting it on the road to replacing the Franc with the euro. Now, with its economic levers curtailed by participation in the single currency, France can only manage its crippling debt by politically risky tax rises or spending cuts.

And Emmanuel Macron? Does he have the political skill required? To Anglo-Saxons weary of maverick leaders, he looked like the statesman they craved. I too admired his square jaw and well-tailored suits, and even (for a brief time) his hauteur. But Granville, like many compatriots, is disappointed. She scoffs at the 'elegantly phrased scripts' of his prepared speeches, and believes he is actively inflaming division in France. Instead of showing empathy with the discontented, he takes their grievances as a personal affront. This, she says, has 'unleashed a vicious circle of mutual alienation between state power and the people'.

Mutual alienation isn't confined to France. It seems to be a feature of the Western world, even in countries where its leaders are less well turned out.

Twenty-first-century Europe has come a long way. Given the horrors of the previous century, on the battlefields and in the death camps, it's little wonder that we focus on making sure they never happen again. Thanks in part to the EU, old foes have learnt the habit of co-operation. Having lost their empires, they no longer compete to rule over the globe. So far, so good.

Yet the danger of rivalry between ruling powers is hardly the only lesson that modern European history teaches. Popular revolt has arguably been as disruptive as inter-state conflict. We ignore the lesson at our peril.

In the sixteenth century, after Martin Luther pinned his Ninety-five Theses to the church door at Wittenberg and translated the Bible from Latin to German, people all over Europe declared a direct link to God, and attacked the authority of the Catholic Church. The Reformation shattered (for a time) a corrupt and intrusive religious hierarchy, profoundly altering the distribution of power. The French Revolution, which drew much of Europe into its orbit, targeted the clergy too, but didn't stop there; it also felled France's aristocracy and its monarchy, via the guillotine.

Revolt is often contagious: 1848 saw rebellions against the established orders in France, Prussia, Italy – indeed most of Continental Europe. In *Revolutionary Spring*, the historian Christopher Clark draws ominous parallels between 1848 and the present. In each nation, a sizeable group felt ignored, their interests neglected by the rulers. In each case, their discontent found expression in revolution.

Then as now, Britain was an outlier. In part this was because, having decapitated its king two centuries earlier, political power was already more diffuse. In part it was because, whenever the authorities got wind of unrest – Chartists campaigning for universal suffrage – they clamped down hard; they'd seen what happened to Charles I.

In November 2018, after a hike in the price of fuel, people began to gather on the outskirts of unassuming French towns to protest. At first they came daily, organising online, then weekly. At its peak, a quarter of a million people joined in, many wearing the high-visibility vests from which the movement took its name. Sometimes the protest turned violent, involving running battles with the heavy-handed police. Over time – the unrest lasted two years – many other grievances were aired: among them poor transport and the disappearance of local services and shops.

Brigitte Granville observes that the '*gilets jaunes*' were people who had become invisible to the system. In their high-vis jackets, they demanded attention. Like many drawn to the MAGA movement in the US, they craved social recognition as well as a better standard of living. She sees them as 'a salutary jolt' to stagnation in French society caused by the country's 'self-perpetuating and self-congratulatory class'.

This element was doubtless present in the Brexit vote too: people tired of being directed from on high, who in voting to 'take back control', wanted more of a say. Judging by developments in Eastern and Central Europe, this appears to be a broadly based sentiment, a backlash against a liberal order that presents its own interests and preferences as self-evidently right.

In many ways, EU enlargement to the East has been a resounding success. Prosperity has risen in the formerly Communist states and they are fully integrated into the EU's institutional framework. Polish, Hungarian, Slovakian and Latvian members of the European Parliament vote and debate, shuffling dutifully between Brussels and Strasbourg to take their places in the peripatetic assembly.

Yet the language of 'enlargement' hints at the problem: a bigger pie doesn't necessarily mean more for everyone. Sure enough, while the GDP of these countries may have risen, they also feel more unequal and divided as societies. Many people resent the corruption they see, the redistribution of public property into the hands of a few. In a number of these countries, a strong illiberalism has taken hold.

In *The Light that Failed*, the Bulgarian thinker Ivan Krastev and his American colleague Stephen Holmes observe that, having idealised what the West stood for throughout the Cold War, these new EU states were initially euphoric to become Western liberal democracies. Over time though, this same liberal democracy came to feel tainted: events like the 2008 financial crash bred a deep distrust of Western elites.

In order to meet the conditions for EU membership, candidate nations were required to adopt policies developed by others. And this was under the guise of governing themselves – of being 'democratised'. Elections felt similarly false; voters might throw out the incumbents, 'but the policies – formulated in Brussels – didn't change'. The last straw, say Krastev and Holmes, was 'being disparaged by visiting Westerners', critical of how they were running things.

All of this 'stoked fears of cultural erasure'. It bred 'politically exploitable longings' for a lost authenticity. And exploited it has been, especially in Orban's Hungary and in Poland, where the illiberal Law and Justice Party (PiS) retain a large and dedicated following.

A key factor in the appeal of these parties, according to Krastev and Holmes, has been the massive flow of people out of the region after the Berlin Wall came down in 1989. The loss of the skilled, the educated, and the young had a profound effect – economically, politically and psychologically too. Money was sent back, but it didn't make up for the absence of these dynamic people who, living abroad, were (and are) not participating in the life of the countries they came from.

*

This echoes my own sense of Poland, which I first visited aged eighteen, when a moral purpose united the country – acting through the movement Solidarity – aiming to regain dignity and shake off the Communist yoke. In the 1980s, I went to teach English at the Catholic Institute for Blind Children in Laski, just outside Warsaw. Marta spoke excellent English and took me under her wing. When Pope John Paul II visited his home country, she took me to his open-air mass in Warsaw stadium, clutching my arm urgently as she translated his deeply political messages about truth and self-respect. When the security services murdered a young, Solidarity-supporting priest, I went with Marta to his parish church in Żoliborz, where thousands of supporters crammed together and lit candles in memory and in protest.

Now she supports Law and Justice. When I recently visited, Żolibosz church was empty, its doors pasted with pictures of foetuses and exhortations about the sanctity of human life. Most of my Polish friends from that time now live abroad, though two of their elderly mothers still live in Warsaw. They too support Law and Justice. The reason, their offspring explain apologetically, is a pension increase credited to that party.

My son Theo's girlfriend, Dominika, is Polish. Her parents did well as commercial lawyers when investment flowed into Poland. Both are liberal minded and patriotic. For well-to-do Poles, deciding where to educate their children poses a dilemma. Swayed ultimately by the belief that fluent English would stand them in good stead, they sent their two daughters to be educated in the UK, where both now live. London's gain is Warsaw's loss, but, without fail at election time, they join the lengthy queue outside the Polish Embassy at Portland Place to cast their votes.

In his book, *The New Politics of Poland*, Jarosław Kuisz has an illuminating take on the fault lines in this long-beleaguered nation. The essential fact, he says, is that there was no Poland from 1795 to 1918. The empires of Russia, Prussia and Austria each helped themselves to a portion, until the entire country was partitioned between them. Poland was wiped off the map. In 1919, the Treaty of Versailles formally restored its nationhood, but this ended in 1939 when Hitler invaded. After the war the country fell under Soviet control, behind the Iron Curtain.

This loss and regaining of sovereignty, Kuisz says, has had a powerful impact on all contemporary politics in Poland, creating a kind of 'post-traumatic sovereignty'. On the one hand, this is what drives the enthusiasm for EU integration, advocated by Donald Tusk's Civic Platform. Being anchored firmly in the West feels to Polish liberals like a bulwark against Russia, which has always sought to subjugate and dominate them, and is today trying to redraw post-Cold War borders. Yet the very same historical experience also informs the rival Law and Justice Party, which declares itself hostile to all outside interference in Poland's affairs, no matter whether it emanates from Moscow or Brussels.

Migration and asylum is another issue that fuels resentment in the East. On 24 August 2015, Angela

Merkel decided to admit hundreds of thousands of Syrian refugees into Germany. Ten days later, Poland, Hungary, the Czech Republic and Slovakia declared the EU quota system for distributing refugees across Europe 'unacceptable'. Krastev and Holmes identify Merkel's decision to 'roll out the red carpet to cultural diversity', as it was seen in sceptical circles, as the point when Central Europe's populists declared their 'independence not only from Brussels but also, more dramatically, from Western liberalism and its religion of openness to the world'.

There is a fear in the region that unassimilable foreigners will dilute national identity and weaken national cohesion. Interestingly, these are countries with no significant immigrant populations. Some suggest that depopulation itself may be behind this sharp sense of loss, in nations that otherwise seem in many ways to have benefited from the post-Communist change.

In April 2024, former Italian prime minister Enrico Letta's eagerly awaited stock-take of the single market was published – a report entitled 'Much More than a Market'. The report contains much of importance, not least, as its title suggest, it underlines a fact over-looked in the UK, that the single market is a political project. The report also repeats an orthodoxy of EU policy that enabling the free movement of people is good because it allows labour to move from areas of unemployment to places where labour is needed. This works as a kind of safety valve within the eurozone, absorbing what Letta calls 'asymmetric shocks'. Yet as Letta's report shows, the EU is also, belatedly, acknowledging that large movements of people can have serious downsides for both the receiving and sending states.

To address the problems in suddenly depopulated countries, Letta has some detailed proposals. He suggests creating a Commission vice-president for a 'Freedom to Stay', and introducing a 'Talent Booster Mechanism' to support regions depleted of people or locked in 'development traps'. This is surreal: elaborate and costly new structures, managed from the centre, to mitigate long-standing problems created by the centre's own inflexibility. No matter what negative consequences it entails, this suggests the free movement of people is sacrosanct.

The sense of alienation felt in Eastern Europe is echoed in East Germany, according to Katja Hoyer. In *Beyond the Wall*, she identifies a similar sense of inferiority – erasure – felt by those from the East after German reunification. It was such a complex experience, and so complete an absorption, she says, that many from the former GDR (German Democratic Republic) don't use the Western term 'reunification'. They say *Wende*: change or turning point.

Before rising under the wing of Helmut Kohl to become Germany's chancellor, Angela Merkel spent her first thirty-one years in the East. She spoke of how this period in the GDR was only ever excused, never embraced. It was part of a past best forgotten.

Kohl ushered in the euro, but Merkel handled the euro crisis. Five countries were bailed out during the crisis and fiscal discipline (austerity) was imposed across the EU. In

Germany she claimed her monetary policy overall was *'alternativlos'* (without alternative). Not everyone agreed. The *Alternatif für Deutschland* (AfD) party began as a eurosceptic party opposed to the euro, and has developed a large following in the east of the country. Strong opposition to immigration is a prominent feature of its electoral platform.

In the 2021 elections, many in the former GDR turned against mainstream political parties. Yet instead of dialogue, they met with derision. Hoyer says their anger doesn't mean that these are people 'lost to democracy', only that 'the system isn't working for them'. She makes the point that German 'reunification is no more the end of history than unification was in 1871'. The GDR might have been absorbed into the structures of the Federal Republic of Germany and the EU, but many feel that their past has been negated. It would be more constructive, says Hoyer, to see reunification as a *Wende* – the start of a process that allows a 'fluid, open, and changeable interpretation of a country which no longer exists'.

Germany is hardly alone in its woes. Italy became a unified state in 1870, but it struggles to maintain a cohesive national identity. Even the slightest acquaintance with the country reveals strong regional differences. The influence of the Austro-Hungarian Empire is palpable on northern cities like Trieste. Ruled by a succession of often distant powers – Spanish, Bourbon, Hapsburg – Naples seems strongly resistant to central control. To say nothing of Sicily.

Italian politics have long been unstable: fascism took hold in the 1920s and '30s, and after the war, many feared that Communism would replace it. Membership of the supranational EU is therefore embraced by many as a way to subsume national dysfunction. European institutions seem to compensate for ineffective national ones.

I recently met up with my Italian friend, Alessandra, in Milan. In the 1990s, we worked as lawyers in the same building in Brussels – she for an American firm, me for a European one. Now she lives in Italy and until recently worked for the Central Bank of Italy, Banca d'Italia. One evening in a small restaurant near her apartment, we found ourselves talking about Europe, despite my intention to steer clear of the topic. Suddenly irritated by the thought of seemingly unstoppable integration, I exclaimed, 'I hate European federalism.'

'I love European federalism,' she replied. 'Europe is my home!' Luckily, we have known each other a long time; we laughed and resumed sipping the excellent (Italian) wine.

Polls regularly find respect for political parties in Italy to be among the lowest in Europe. Historically, more than any other country, it has spurned its politicians, appointing technocratic leaders – perceived to be experts – to steer the country instead. Between 1993 and 2021, it was led by four different technocratic leaders, each brought in by constitutional mechanisms rather than elections.

Yet having expert knowledge is not the same as being able to take effective political decisions. Technocracy has a different function, in some ways opposed to pluralistic politics. Democracy is about finding an accommodation between different views and approaches; technocracy assumes that there is one solution to any problem, a right answer that the expert knows and will implement. Every state needs experts to support it, of course. The danger arises when they assume too much power. By sidelining democracy, the essential link with the people is broken. Policies that don't command support are enacted, provoke confrontation, and are then abandoned (or worse, not abandoned). This destroys faith in the system and may prompt a backlash.

Fascism and xenophobia – hallmarks of the Third Reich and Mussolini's Italy – gave the nation state itself a bad name. At the end of the war, the desire to build a post-national world took root, and efforts were made to eradicate nationalism altogether. Germany, of course, embraced this cosmopolitan project with particular zeal, lodging itself firmly in the supranational EU.

As Hans Kundnani sees it, however, within the EU the corollary of idealising European identity has been to demonise national identity. Given Germany's history, it is understandable that Germans would see nationalism as a dark, elemental force, springing from hatred of the Other. But this also creates blind spots. It obscures the 'emancipatory aspects' of nationalism, Kundnani says, and negates its anti-colonial projects, such as India's fight for independence.

In Central and Eastern Europe, nationalism was also experienced quite differently. Many countries in the region were created in 1919 from the Austro-Hungarian and Ottoman empires, propelled into existence by their very desire for nationhood. In the same places, more recently, it was again their strong sense of the nation – nationalism – that made Soviet domination so intolerable and fuelled their own independence struggles. Poland is a stark example, but by no means alone.

Since the pandemic and large-scale migration brought back borders, the European dream of a post-national world has been fading. But rather than bemoan this fact, there is a strong case for embracing national feeling. After all, it is real and it is enduring.

Many countries celebrate a national day. Typically, it will mark the founding of the nation or a significant event in its history; apart from enjoying a day off work, people need a story to bind them together. In France, it is the storming of the Bastille on 14 July, which marked a climax of the revolution and led to the founding of the republic. In Germany it is 3 October – German Unity Day, the anniversary of reunification (the *Wende*) in 1990. Norwegians mark the signing of their constitution on 17 May 1814. Poland's official national day is 11 November, commemorating the restoration of its sovereignty in 1918, although a different day gets out the crowds and parades: 15 August. In 1920, over two weeks, Polish forces fought back and overcame the Red Army, halting the advance of Communism into Europe. The Soviet side had looked so overwhelming that Poland's victory is remembered as the Miracle on the Vistula.

The UK doesn't have a national day as such, though the royal family provides plenty of birthdays, jubilees and coronations to celebrate. Remembrance Sunday – with its service and wreath-laying at the cenotaph – is a national and Commonwealth event. Sadly the fifth of November, commemorating Guy Fawkes's failed Gunpowder Plot, has fallen into abeyance. I suppose it isn't thought nice to burn Catholics even in effigy, though personally I am fond of a bonfire. And there's a pleasing ambivalence at the heart of this event. Are we celebrating – with explosions and rockets – that Parliament was saved, or wistfully imagining what would have been?

Today, the dangers of xenophobic nationalism are understood. But nationalism has a benign aspect, and ignoring national feeling – people's sense of their heritage, contested as that may be – leaves an opening for extremists to exploit. As Europe absorbs newcomers migrating from different parts of the world, it may even be that its nations need a unifying story more than ever.

In a similar way, the European project has sought to dilute the sovereignty of nations in general. This is a mistake. There is much to commend the national state as a unit of solidarity, well suited to the modern need for civic responsibility and active political participation. Responsible for the well-being of its citizens, it is also generally small enough to be held to account. In a world where many institutions that used to bind people together no longer do – the Church, political parties, trade unions, the army – it may be that the nation state, with its 'community of memory' as Tony Judt called it, and its 'familiar and appropriately scaled frame', is the best remaining source of communal identity.

Attempts have been made to create a sense of community and solidarity at European level. In 1985, the EU co-opted a flag from the Council of Europe and its anthem 'Ode to Joy'. This is meaningful for some of us, but I fear the appeal is limited. People are capable of multiple allegiances and identities. Broadly speaking, though, Judt is surely right that 'Europe is too large and nebulous a concept around which to forge any convincing human community'.

There are, of course, problems with nation states. They can be exclusive. Multinational ones risk breaking up, as in Yugoslavia. Minorities may try to acquire territories at someone else's expense. Or, as in Ukraine, their right to exist at all may be contested, and the presence of a minority, alleged to be persecuted, used as a pretext to intervene.

Ukraine became independent from the collapsing Soviet Union on 24 August 1991, but Vladimir Putin has increasingly challenged its sovereignty. At the time of writing, Russia now occupies 20 per cent of Ukraine's territory.

This poses profound questions for Europe. The EU is a significant trading bloc, but it has little geopolitical clout and no autonomous military capability to speak of. A Russian invasion on its doorstep catapulted the issue of defence high up the political agenda. And with the US no longer willing to pay, that pushes it right to the top.

Since the start of the Cold War, the North Atlantic Treaty Organisation has guaranteed European security under American leadership. With thirty European and two North Atlantic members (the US and Canada), NATO has been an undoubted success as a military alliance, lately boosted by the arrival of Sweden and Finland in response to the Russian invasion.

But the US military presence in our part of the world was only ever intended to be temporary – a stopgap until Europe's economies were stronger. As far back as 1959, President Eisenhower complained that the US was carrying practically the whole weight of the strategic defence force, conducting space programmes, paying for infrastructure and maintaining large naval and air forces in Europe. The Europeans, he said famously, are close to 'making a sucker out of Uncle Sam'. President Obama diplomatically made the same point. Now – forcefully – it is the turn of the Trump administration. With Russia waging war in Europe, and China flexing its muscles in the Indo-Pacific, Europe knows it must act.

What this means, first of all, is having a visible military capability and demonstrated willingness to use it. The first Trump administration chastised European allies who failed to spend 2 per cent of GDP on defence, in line with NATO's guideline. Today, the agreed target is 5 per cent.

For many European countries, including the UK, meeting this will be an enormous political challenge, given the multiple demands on the public purse. As former defence secretary Ben Wallace points out, the UK has been slipping in the NATO ranking for military investment. Germany, historically a low spender, has amended its constitution to permit a bigger defence budget (removing the 'debt brake'). Among European NATO allies, Poland is now the top spender. It is also introducing conscription, and other European countries are rearming. According to the *Economist*, in Vilnius, Lithuania, the public recently welcomed German tanks as part of a NATO exercise, untroubled by the memory of Nazi occupation. Some of the assembled German dignitaries were the ones who seemed a bit spooked.

Britain and France are Europe's only nuclear military powers. They are both permanent members of the Security Council and co-operate closely and well, an arrangement formalised in the Lancaster House Treaties. This will continue, but many consider they both need to work more closely with Poland and Germany, too. The UK's 2024 Trinity House Agreement with Germany is a move in this direction, as is a new UK–Poland treaty.

The UK's position remains 'NATO first'. The way to counter Russia and strengthen European security, the UK believes, is with greater European leadership in

NATO, and enhanced nuclear, new-tech and modern conventional weapons capabilities. To support this approach, Britain intends to build on the bilateral defence agreements and regional groupings that already exist in Europe. This works well with Norway, Italy and Turkey, for example, and through the Joint Expeditionary Force in northern Europe and the Baltic.

It's worth underlining the fact that the EU has no command structure capable of running an operation to defend a member state. (It was, after all, set up to make war impossible.) Under the aegis of the European External Action Service, it conducts small non-combat missions outside the EU (such as training missions in Mozambique and Somalia). Otherwise, it 'borrows' from NATO, for example to conduct peacekeeping operations in Bosnia and Herzegovina.

Despite this constitutional tendency to pacifism, the EU has a vital role to play in strengthening Europe's defence capability. That role is helping states to fund the increase in spending, whether by the use of euro bonds or by creating a dedicated rearmament bank (an option the UK supports). The EU can also do much to co-ordinate and rationalise defence procurement: the existing fragmented approach is thought to waste billions.

According to UK defence policy, NATO, however, should remain the military planning body. As David Owen puts it, 'War fighting requires a military organisation with a clear command and control procedure. It cannot be fitted into an EU of twenty-seven countries.

Procurement can be a collective EU decision; war fighting simply cannot be.'

It is likely that the US will draw down some troops and NATO personnel. Here the Europeans will also need to step up. France has historically strained against American military leadership. In 1966, President de Gaulle withdrew France from NATO's integrated command structure. It returned in 2009, although its nuclear deterrent remains independent. President Macron – a self-proclaimed Gaullist – picked up the baton by advocating 'strategic autonomy'. He rightly acknowledged that Europe had to shoulder a greater defence burden and reduce dependence on the US, questioning its 'commitment' to the Continent. However, for all the talk, France's military spending has remained static and in 2023 it did not even meet NATO's 2 per cent target.

Reports that France wished to confine access to a new €150 billion fund (known as Security Action for Europe or SAFE) to European defence companies were discouraging. This kind of protectionism should be resisted: it seems wiser for Europe to buy whatever does the job best. Detail about a UK–EU 'comprehensive security and defence agreement', allegedly concluded in May, is hard to come by. It was said to have been held up by French demands over fish. The security of Europe is paramount and shouldn't be determined by fractious French fishermen.

As the defence secretary, John Healey, has written, the war in Ukraine shows that 'a nation's Armed Forces are only as strong as the industry, innovators and investors that stand behind them'. Technological innovation is vital to stay ahead of adversaries.

This extends to Europe's nuclear capability. China told Russia it would support the invasion of Ukraine as long as they guaranteed they would *not* use nuclear weapons. Yet as David Owen pointed out to me, Russian forces in Europe do in fact have battlefield nuclear weapons and believe in their early use. This is reflected in some of their war-fighting documents, and is often advocated by senior Russian politician, Dmitry Medvedev.

There is, Owen says, a 'huge responsibility' to rapidly enhance European nuclear capability – involving the UK and France working closely with Germany and Poland – within the terms of the Non-Proliferation Treaty. This is, of course, a terrifying prospect, but reality requires us to be armed and prepared.

While the slaughter in Ukraine continues, the EU has opened accession talks and is committed, on paper at least, to welcoming Ukraine as a member. Naturally, Ukraine's President, Volodymyr Zelensky, sees this as a lifeline. In reality, there are so many obstacles to accession that, if it happens at all, it won't be soon.

The EU's default position is to enlarge. Its official line is that geopolitically the EU 'needs' to do this, to keep candidate countries in the Balkans and south-west within its sphere of influence, rather than that of Russia. Yet some candidates, such as Turkey, have been in the waiting room for so long that they have become restive and resentful. Public opinion in Albania, too, has cooled on the idea of joining the club.

This suggests that the EU needs a better way to relate to its neighbours, one not solely focused on membership. The same, I would argue, applies to how it manages its relations with the UK, a large and globally influential former member.

In 2023, a Franco-German-led study commissioned by the EU to look at enlargement came to a stark conclusion. Taking on new members, it found, would require far-reaching reform – without which the EU would fail, paralysed by an inability to take collective decisions. 'The EU is not ready yet to welcome new members,' it declared, 'neither institutionally nor policy wise.'

Many interesting points are raised in this paper, titled 'Sailing on High Seas: Reforming and Enlarging the EU for the 21st Century', but perhaps the most significant is that it formally moots the idea of a multi-speed Europe. This would mean an institutional structure – or series of structures – with varying levels, or speeds, of integration. Such mechanisms have been proposed before. Multi-speed Europe, concentric circles, variable geometry: all these phrases were in vogue at one time or other. But it is important that they are now back.

For the UK, they present a significant opportunity. It was precisely the EU's 'one-size-fits-all' model that fed British discontent and led it to leave the union. On its way out, the UK was (and still is) often criticised by Brussels for 'cherry picking' the parts of the European project that it favours. A multi-speed Europe makes this language redundant. It means creating bespoke arrangements among different countries. This inevitably involves picking cherries.

The reality is that neither we nor the EU can carry on as we were. The need to credibly deter aggression – whether from Russia or other authoritarian powers – and fight should that become necessary, means that better co-operation between the UK and our European partners is an imperative. Regardless of EU membership, it is essential to ensure the European industrial base can produce what Europe needs to defend itself, at affordable prices and in sufficient quantities.

All advanced democracies are under strain. The relationship with the US will continue to be challenging. But though Europe's military dependency on the US must end, it is plainly in Europe's interests to keep the US engaged in a transatlantic alliance.

None of this will be possible without achieving greater social and political cohesion. As the UK's Strategic Defence Review observes, change of the necessary magnitude requires a 'whole-of-society' response. That in turn will need us to address a range of popular grievances: improving how the state functions and appealing to unifying sentiments, at both the national and supranational levels, without turning on an internal enemy. It means doing politics better and being willing to embrace radical possibilities.

Chapter Four

Another Europe Is Possible

Under a clear sky, guests make their way past the EU delegation's headquarters in Smith Square, a short walk from the Palace of Westminster. The building was once Conservative Central Office. Many know it from an image of Mrs Thatcher after her 1987 election victory, Britain's first female prime minister, resplendent in pearls and with shiny set hair waving at supporters from the window.

Walking up the steps of St John's – a concert hall, once a church in the square's centre – I attach an entwined EU flag and Union Jack pin to my lapel.

It's 9 May, 2025. A hundred or so guests are gathered to celebrate Europe Day. This year also marks seventy-five years since the Schuman Plan was signed in 1950. We are celebrating Europe coming together, after conflict almost destroyed it, and we are celebrating the EU's continuing bond with the UK. People here speak of the shock and grief of our leaving. Others talk about ongoing problems such as transporting artworks across borders. There is realism among the EU delegation, and a determination to work closely together. Nowadays there are fewer formal meetings, they say, but many contacts about joint problems and programmes, at all levels. Many of these Europeans have lived happily here for a long time.

After milling around for a while, the orchestra strikes up. From a gallery above, singers pelt out the EU's anthem, the 'Ode to Joy', and I find myself a little choked up. Nostalgia, for what Britain has lost? Or simply for my childhood at the European School? By 2016, I felt we had run out of road, but I will always mourn that we couldn't bridge our differences. *'Alle werden Brüder sein':* the ideal of universal brotherhood has deep emotional appeal.

That weekend, Britons also gathered to celebrate eighty years since the end of the war: Victory in Europe Day. The royal family lined the balcony of Buckingham Palace, craning their necks as twenty-three military aircraft flew past, ending with nine Red Arrows, rending the air.

A minute earlier they had flown over my house in East London. Many people came out to watch and record them on their phones. Some consider this ritual too militaristic. I don't. My father's brother was killed on an RAF base at the start of the Battle of Britain. He was nineteen. It feels right that little Prince George shakes hands in gratitude with a wheelchair-bound veteran. Neither does it feel insular: it honours all those – Brits, Poles, Czechs, Canadians, Americans and many others – who defended Britain and liberated occupied Europe. And today, amid renewed threats to European security and government calls for a 'whole-of-society' response, the need to engender a spirit of quiet resolve is once again real.

On Europe Day, there was an air of anticipation about the UK–EU reset, which Labour had been trailing for months. The plan, it said, was to stick to the red lines but get something better than the 'flawed' TCA negotiated by the previous government. Anticipating this, the well-connected think tank, Centre for European Reform (CER), set out what it considered the obstacles to closer relations and what lay behind the perceived lack of 'ambition'. It said that to progress, both sides would have to be willing to abandon orthodoxies and red lines.

From the EU side, it noted a sense that Britain shouldn't be seen to flourish and a reluctance to give something to Britain which other third countries would want too. And the UK, it was said, 'needs to work to re-establish trust'.

Undoubtedly, for all the determination to work together, there is still bitterness. This obviously limits what is on offer today. However, I would suggest that the demands of the present mean it is time to discard the notion that the UK needs to atone for the past.

The negotiations around exit were tough. David Cameron, as PM, forbade the civil service from planning for a Leave vote, fearing this would give the option credibility. So, yes, the UK was unprepared for such a complex and involved set of negotiations. And the vote did not dictate the nature of our future relationship – there were many competing options. We were profoundly divided. This allowed Brussels to set the terms and tie us in knots, particularly over the border in Ireland.

In 2021–2022, in the face of severe trade dislocation between Britain and Northern Ireland, and resulting community tension, the EU stood firm. It repeated that this was a problem of the UK's own making and that the terms being implemented had been agreed. The EU played hardball. It was entitled to do so. It may have succeeded in intimidating others, but it did not promote good relations. Both sides bear the scars.

Trust is a nebulous thing. But here are some facts.

For over forty years, the UK was an engaged and effective member of the EU. It was a driving force in two of the EU's most significant achievements: the creation of the single market and enlargement to the East. It had an excellent record of implementing EU law, seeking guidance from the ECJ and complying with court judgments. For many years, it was one of only two net contributors to the EU budget. It was, and I would say still is, a good European.

Outside the EU, the UK is steadily finding its feet.

HM Treasury forecasts of economic disaster consequent on a vote to leave – an immediate recession and 500–800,000 unemployed – plainly did not come about. The actual economic impact of leaving remains contested, and this is unlikely to change: the pandemic, rising energy costs, changes in how trade is recorded, all made it difficult to identify cause and effect. An often-quoted

Office of Budget Responsibility (OBR) forecast of 4 per cent loss of GDP consequent on leaving the EU is challenged over its underlying assumptions. Furthermore, the 'forecast' doesn't attempt to factor in future changes to the economic or regulatory environment, whether in the UK or abroad.

Another body of opinion posits that the UK's performance has remained relatively constant pre- and post-leaving the EU, implying that the economic picture is neutral. The former *FT* columnist, Wolfgang Münchau, falls into this camp. Writing now for *UnHerd*, he says that 'from an economic perspective . . . Brexit was a non-event'. The single market, he says, is 'not what it says on the label'. It produced growth in 1992, but since then has become hampered by a 'thicket of rules and regulations'. Since it is not a genuine single market, he says, leaving wasn't a shock.

Again, Dyson's experience seems to echo this. 'Selling products into the so-called single market,' he told me, 'often feels like shipping to twenty-seven different countries. We are forced to juggle different plug shapes, languages and repack the same product to satisfy a bureaucratic maze of national rules on labelling, packaging, "repairability" and more. The result is chaos – with almost as much energy spent on negotiating bureaucracy as on innovation.'

That said, there is little doubt that selling goods into such a heavily regulated market has created friction on the UK–EU border.

The UK maintains high food safety and other phytosanitary standards, but the EU will not recognise these, and demands compliance with its own. Proving compliance requires the production of certificates and other copious paperwork, which creates costs and delay. Larger companies have adapted, but many smaller businesses – artisan cheese producers, for example – have struggled. Some have given up on export, or gone out of business.

On the brighter side, there has never really been a single market in services, and it is services, rather than goods, that make up the heart of the UK economy. Law, insurance, financial services, consulting, retail, leisure and culture make up 80 per cent of its economic output. Since leaving the EU, British trade in services has thrived, as has overall trade with the rest of world.

The City no longer seeks closer ties with the EU. Thanks to technologically enabled innovation and its expansion into new growth areas, like fin tech, digital currencies and green finance, it is doing well. The UK is likely, therefore, to continue to diverge from the EU in how it regulates its global financial services market.

More slowly perhaps than many would like, the UK is replacing other EU regimes with its own: procurement, competition, subsidy control. And it is refining its approach to regulation – not by doing away with existing rules, but developing a more streamlined, nimble approach, as shown by the Medicines and Healthcare Regulatory Authority (MHRA) swiftly approving vaccines during the pandemic.

The UK is also building trading relationships in new parts of the world, where growth is strong. In December 2024, it joined the Comprehensive and Progressive Agreement for Trans-Pacific Partnership (CPTPP), which creates a free-trade zone with eleven other countries in the Asia–Pacific region. In 2025 it concluded a trade agreement with India – forecast to be the fourth-largest world economy by 2028 – which would not have been possible as a member of the EU.

Writing in *The Times*, a former French diplomat, François-Joseph Schichan, observed:

> Post-Brexit Britain is doing just fine . . . The argument that it would be left without any influence internationally after leaving the EU has been disproved on trade, foreign policy, innovation and many other areas; the UK is a global actor and will remain one. Recent trade deals with the US and India undermine a fundamental EU argument: that negotiating as a bloc gets you better results than individual negotiations.

There are, in short, grounds to be confident and optimistic. Moreover, a spirit of optimism can itself be an economic asset. We are entering a revolution in science and technology. To flourish, a developed economy like ours needs to be nimble and able to adapt quickly to grasp new opportunities. A consensus about where some of these opportunities might lie has been emerging and is usefully set out in a joint report, 'A New National Purpose: Innovation Can Power the Future of Britain' by Tony Blair and William Hague – senior former leaders of opposing political parties. Biotech, clean energy and AI are all identified as targets for growth. To these, defence should probably be added.

The EU also sees these as important sectors for future growth. But according to voices inside the EU, its strategic approach will need to change radically if it wants to seize such opportunities.

In 2008, the US and Eurozone economies were roughly the same size. Today the US economy is nearly twice as large. Every state in the US, apart from Mississippi and Idaho, has a higher GDP per person than the EU average.

The EU has created an over-regulated, under-integrated single market that is uncompetitive vis-à-vis its main trading rivals, the US and China. This is the conclusion of two separate studies by former Italian prime ministers, Enrico Letta and Mario Draghi, commissioned by the EU. In his report, 'The Future of European Competitiveness', Draghi finds burdensome regulation holding back innovation. He refers to 'the EU's extensive and stringent regulatory environment' exemplified by policies based on the precautionary principle.

Titanium dioxide is a mineral used to colour food or enhance its whiteness. In 2020, France banned it and, in 2022, the EU followed, applying the precautionary principle. This means acting on a potential threat even in the absence of conclusive scientific evidence of harm. The UK Food Safety Agency undertook its own detailed assessment of risk (available online) and, in the absence of evidence of harm, approved its continued use. You might not be a fan of iced buns (or the erythrosine-treated cherry sitting on the top), but you aren't compelled to eat it, and compulsory labelling identifies any additives. Banning something on a precautionary basis closes the door to innovation, almost by definition.

Münchau agrees that over-regulation is stifling growth. Since the UK left, he says, the EU 'doubled down with regulation for AI, the crypto-industry, for digital markets and for digital services'.

Entrepreneur, former policy advisor to David Cameron and self-confessed Remainer, Rohan Silva, is not impressed by the EU's AI Act. Writing in *The Times* he noted how it was 'breathlessly heralded by European leaders as "the world's first AI legislation"'. But his verdict is stark: 'it's genuinely hard to overstate how dreadful for innovation and growth these rules will be.'

His explanation is detailed, but errors in the Act include clamping down on models in general, rather than specific applications, like deep-fake porn videos, and fixing an 'arbitrary upper limit' on the models' size, despite our having no idea at this early stage how the technology will develop. Although Silva considers the rules to be 'half-witted' and 'barmy', there will be pressure on the UK to follow, he says, and the consequences will be 'monumental'. AI businesses subject to these regulations 'will be hiring lawyers and lobbyists,' he says, 'while Americans recruit software engineers.'

Pressuring those outside the EU to follow EU regulation is an old technique, known as the Brussels effect. Lacking hard power, the EU has historically used stringent regulations to exert economic influence beyond its own borders. In the past, given the size of the EU market, companies outside the EU felt compelled to adopt its standards in areas such as data protection, the use of chemicals, airline emissions and the exploitation of natural resources for all their operations. Yet the efficacy of this tool is decreasing as the EU's economic might declines relative to rivals like the US and China. This kind of take-it-or-leave-it moral leadership only works when leaving it isn't an option. In many parts of the world, from the Asia–Pacific region to Africa, countries now can and do choose to do business with others. And in sectors like AI, where the EU has no real presence (the UK has more AI business than Germany and France combined and almost as much as the whole EU), global standards will be determined elsewhere.

According to Draghi, innovation is also held back by the lack of a business environment that encourages start-ups in cutting-edge sectors. Where support exists through flagship EU programmes such as Horizon, he says, processes are cumbersome and slow.

In 2014 there was a renewed push (spearheaded by the British commissioner in the EU) to create a Capital Markets Union, centred on London, to knit together

Europe's fragmented markets. This never came to pass, and the EU remains hamstrung by the difficulty of mobilising capital to fund and invest in priority areas such as innovation, infrastructure, green energy and now defence. Leveraging private money is especially tough without developed private equity and venture capital markets.

In euro circles, the Letta and Draghi reports are driving policy change. Worries about overburdening business and stifling innovation appear to have prompted something of a regulatory retreat at EU level. The Commission has produced a 'Competitiveness Compass' to improve competitiveness, including by 'drastically' reducing the regulatory and administrative burden, simplifying legislation by repealing what isn't needed. Many Green Deal measures are being shelved, as are rules holding companies liable for harm caused by AI applications and for human rights abuses in their supply chains.

This policy churn at EU level makes it especially difficult to fathom the UK government's apparent commitment to greater alignment with EU regulation.

Starmer's reset is said to commit the UK to an 'SPS Phytosanitary deal' with the EU, whereby the UK would 'dynamically align' with EU rules on food and other agricultural standards. In the absence of detail, most people are left wondering what on earth dynamic alignment is. 'Dynamic' sounds forward-looking, and 'alignment' sounds friendly, so maybe it's good? Maybe. Without reliable data on trade, it's hard to judge. Following existing EU rules on some things will doubtless help some businesses sell more easily into the EU. But at what price?

As things stand – under arrangements that the government appears to have agreed – the UK will have no say in making the rules it must apply. We may think those rules are daft or unnecessary (like the ban on titanium dioxide). No matter. We will have agreed to apply them; and not just to goods for export into the EU, but for all such goods we produce and sell in the UK. So, this might be the end of the bright, white, cherry-topped iced bun.

A pledge to follow EU phytosanitary rules, now and in the future, with no vote on the rules, is bad enough. But to do so at a time when the Commission is reconsidering its approach to regulation and when technology is transforming the sector, seems very unwise. Why commit to adopting a whole raft of rules that could soon be for the bin? New ways of producing food might be healthier, or kinder to animals and the environment. Why shut the door on this possibility?

The government may have very good answers to these questions. If so, it is guarding them closely.

These aren't hypothetical problems.

Hoxton Farms is on my bike route to work, so I stop off to visit. It is next to Hoxton, but it isn't a farm. It is a life science start-up, which grows fat in a lab to create a tasty alternative to meat. Its co-founder, Ed Steele, explains that as a novel food (not sold before 2017), they need regulatory approval before they can sell to consumers.

They are not seeking approval in the EU at this stage, Ed says, because the process would take three to five years. Also, the issue is becoming politicised. In the UK, the Genetic Technology (Precision Breeding) Act 2023 gives a green light to the process and there is a move to push novel foods. On the Continent, opposition from traditional agriculture seems to be growing. Italy has banned cultivated meat, although the Commission are opposing this. Regulatory approval from the domestic Food Standards Agency is still arduous, but Ed feels it is improving, and there is progress towards a system better suited to new products like theirs. The company works with the regulator as they develop the product. If something is considered a problem, they adapt it.

He is also positive about the UK's new research funding agency, ARIA (Advanced Research and Invention Agency), which bridges the gap between science and new businesses and helps find private sources of funding. It works, Ed says, by staying outside of government bureaucracy. It is run by scientists and innovators rather than civil servants, and deliberately avoids imposing too much top-down control. Start-up culture is more comfortable with risk: out of twenty or so projects, maybe only two to three will succeed. This is too low a hit rate for taxpayer's money.

In 2024, Ed and his co-founder Max considered

setting up a production facility in the US, but its newly uncertain regulatory environment made them alter their plans. Instead, they are looking at Singapore and Japan, where, Ed says, British companies have a good reputation on food safety and ethics. I mention the Trans-Pacific Partnership, the trade agreement that the UK recently joined, expecting Ed to look blank. Yes, he says, it does make a difference. They want the trade and are willing to offer practical help to secure it.

As we walk to the labs, I learn that the company employs fifty people of thirty nationalities, twenty of whom have PhDs. This means new Home Office restrictions on visas, including raised income thresholds for 'migrants', are a concern. Inside a lab, I tiptoe gingerly in elasticated blue cover shoes, and peer into a fridge where a large look-alike salami sausage is hanging. 'Isn't it a bit . . . animally?' I ask unscientifically. There are three things, apparently, that trouble meat-avoiders: health, animal ethics and climate. 'We tick all those boxes,' Ed says.

Before leaving the buzzing communal space, I ask whether aligning with EU phytosanitary rules will affect what they do. Ed says they have tried to find out, but it seems nobody knows.

If companies like this are prevented from developing, it would seem a terrible own goal.

Cycling on to work I muse on the future of food. In sci-fi films I watched as a child, food in the twenty-first century became purely functional: potions in packs or a pill, like what was eaten in space. But Ed and Max clearly love food. Explaining how the company started, Ed described enjoying the rituals of family meals, and taking pleasure in traditional dishes passed down generations. He also spoke about his and Max's interest in science and maths, and an obsession – which became Hoxton Farms – with what happens when you manipulate the molecules in various foodstuffs. And why not?

Climate change is ravaging Africa, and in many places sustenance remains scarce. Every day, thousands of desperate people uproot themselves and travel north, looking for better chances in life. But anxieties about food shortages extend much further afield. According to Ed, clients in the Far East frequently cite food security as a driver for interest in their product: the taste of meat without having to buy, and rear, the cow (as it were).

If technological innovation can give us what we need more cheaply, more reliably, and more ethically, it's hard to defend a regulatory system that does anything other than make sure the products are safe. That's the sort of dynamism we need. Anything else is fiddling while the fields burn. With the EU chocolate directive, the fiddling lasted twenty-seven years. But as the planet heats up, we don't have that kind of time.

On the other hand, EU time is a peculiar thing: watch for long enough and you could swear that the past is repeating itself.

In the early 1990s, after the Berlin Wall fell and the federalists' dream to create a single currency suddenly became possible, the European project was at a crossroads. The UK encouraged enlargement to the East, a process described as 'widening' the EU, which some felt was favoured by the UK as a way of preventing its 'deepening' – integrating within a monetary union. There was talk then of a 'multi-speed' Europe: different countries could choose how far they wished to go with integration, and the Community structure would reflect that. But the idea got lost. In the event, the EU simultaneously widened and deepened.

After monetary union, with the eurozone in crisis, similar ideas resurfaced. In 2012, David Owen, the former Labour rebel and foreign secretary, published a book called *Restructuring Europe* in which he proposed a version of the project that separated out a wide and a deep structure, side by side. The deep structure would be a full European Union, working supranationally – with all the political integration necessary to allow the single currency to function. The wide structure would comprise a looser grouping of countries outside the euro, mainly working inter-governmentally, called the European Community. This would in essence be the single market, but with a new court to decide trade disputes, and many more countries welcomed into the fold.

The plan didn't catch on. Charles Grant, director of the Centre for European Reform (CER), recalls thinking at the time that Owen's suggestions were the musings of a sceptic, and so dismissed them. And governments, it seems, didn't want to appear less than enthusiastic about full membership. No member state wanted to be relegated to a 'slow lane', to be treated as a second-class citizen. This was reflected in British policy (and Grant's thinking, too). In Cameron's 2013 Bloomberg speech, he explicitly rejected talk of different 'speeds', despite having no intention of taking Britain into the euro. Instead of proposing alternative structures, like Owen, he opted to 'renegotiate Britain's relationship' and then call an in/out referendum on membership.

Well, the referendum took us out, so today the picture is different. And there is now a body of opinion in the EU – how large is difficult to gauge – which recognises that one-size-fits-all may not, in fact, fit very many.

In practice, variable geometry already exists. Not all member states are in the euro. Schengen includes some but not all EU states, plus others from outside. Although part of the Schengen area, Denmark is committed to its krone and, as was the case with the UK, has opted out of EU measures covering justice and home affairs, migration and asylum policy. The European Economic Area (EEA) comprises all EU countries plus three others: Iceland, Norway and Liechtenstein, which are also in the European Free Trade Area (EFTA). Turkey is in a customs union with the EU, as well as being a candidate country for membership.

Despite this, the EU orthodoxy, repeated frequently during the negotiations over Britain's exit and parroted faithfully by the press, is that third countries (like the UK) cannot 'cherry-pick' the arrangement with the EU.

A number of recent developments suggest an important shift in approach, even if the fruit-harvesting metaphor hasn't changed.

The first is visible in the EU's agreement with Switzerland, (a non-EU, non-EEA member like Britain), concluded in December 2024. The Swiss are gradually asserting themselves more. An 'Institutional Framework Agreement' drawn up in 2018 was rejected by the Swiss Federal Council, reportedly over concerns about sovereignty and immigration. Displeased, the EU retaliated by limiting Switzerland's ability to offer financial services within the EU and suspended its participation in the scientific research programme, Horizon (as it did with the UK during the dispute over the Northern Ireland Protocol). Now, a new EU–Swiss agreement limits the role of the ECJ in favour of independent arbitration and creates a tailored regime of single market access. The deal envisages Switzerland joining a 'common food safety area', aligning with most, but not all, EU phytosanitary laws. This apparent willingness of the EU to set aside some old orthodoxies is a notable change.

Writing recently in the *Observer*, Enrico Letta, author of the single market report, signalled another tantalising shift. He expressed regret about the loss of impetus for the EU Capital Markets Union after the UK departure, and – more strikingly – regret about *the EU's response* to the departure. 'Rather than rethink the model,' he wrote,

'Europe fell into a struggle over who would take London's place. The question blinded us to the reality: there is no other London' (as far as mobilising capital is concerned). Letta dangles the prospect of UK involvement in a Savings and Investment Union, intended to improve access to private capital within the EU. What kind of future collaboration this could involve isn't addressed. But it indicates a change in the balance of power.

The most explicit recognition that the EU needs a different institutional structure and relationship with its neighbours comes in the discussion over enlargement.

The 'Sailing on High Seas' report about EU enlargement envisages four 'concentric circles': first an inner zone of the eurozone and Schengen; then the EU; then associate members; and finally an outer tier of essentially bilateral relationships along the lines of the existing European Political Community – a grouping of forty-six countries, established in 2022.

Where the UK might fit within this structure will depend on what it wants from a relationship with the EU. None of the concentric circles as currently sketched out would work for the UK – it should not, for example, agree to be a 'rule taker' (which associate membership envisages) without a meaningful role in agreeing those rules. Still, the concept is interesting and could be developed.

What the UK wants will also depend on how the EU itself develops from here. The EU is not standing still. It too is adapting to a turbulent world. And with twenty-seven member states, with different interests, aims and electorates, charting a clear course for the future is a monumental challenge. How far will the eurozone choose to integrate? How will the EU respond to Trump's tariffs? Will it see through the measures proposed in the Draghi report to increase competitiveness or is it too wedded to top-down regulation? Will it find the annual investment of €750–800 billion – 4.5 per cent of EU GDP – that Draghi says is required, or will it settle for a less expensive industrial reorganisation and some ad hoc reform? What recent regulations will it jettison in order to become more competitive? Could it embrace the vision of a multi-speed Europe? All this is up in the air.

When contemplating a closer relationship with the EU, there are other orthodoxies that the UK would need to consider.

The EU's handling of subsidiarity is one. Few people – other than political scientists – are enthused by subsidiarity. It is an ugly word, but the concept itself matters. It means that decisions should be taken as close as possible to where they will take effect. In other words, act locally where possible and centralise only where necessary.

The duty to respect subsidiarity was added to the EU Treaties at member states' insistence, led by the UK, but it is more honoured in the breach than the observance. The institutions see the principle as limiting EU action and therefore to be resisted.

Complaints to the ECJ about its breach rarely meet with success. Catherine Barnard, professor of EU law, notes that historically the court has been unwilling to review the substance of complaints about subsidiarity. Despite member states seeking to give it legal effect by inserting it into the Treaties, the court considered it to be a 'political' principle rather than a legal one – in other words, one it decided it could ignore. Over the years, mechanisms have been crafted to try to address this, but to little avail. In reality, unless the Commission and the ECJ see the point of it, and choose to live by it, this is a fight member states are destined to lose.

When should the EU act? When are laws needed at Community level? An argument can always be advanced that fixing a uniform EU standard or rule will be more effective in creating a level playing field between nations. Leaving aside the desirability of adopting international standards, is it always necessary to level the playing field? In all areas? At any cost? Genuinely applying the principle of subsidiarity requires grasping the value of proximity in itself. Viewed from the Berlaymont building in Brussels or ministries in national capitals, local action often looks disorganised and inefficient, so the centre is reluctant to relinquish control. Yet local action, supported by those it will affect, often will be more effective. There is a civic dimension to this. Democracy works when citizens participate and feel they have a decent level of control over their lives.

Subsidiarity is linked to decentralisation. At a national

level, we seem to grasp why this matters. In the UK, both main political parties have agreed that locally elected mayors – particularly for big cities – are a good thing. In their book *Head North: A Rallying Cry for a More Equal Britain*, Andy Burnham and Steve Rotheram argue (as mayors of Manchester and Liverpool respectively) that more political power should be channelled north from Westminster. Westminster seems reluctant to actually do that, but at least it pays lip service to the justice of their cause. Why, then, is the same principle not insisted upon where the EU is concerned?

This isn't just a UK thing. Brigitte Granville sees decentralisation as a partial remedy to what ails France. Recentring the country on its 'component localities', she says, will give 'what social scientists call greater "agency", while poets might call it a chance to breathe a freer air' in a country where people are 'gasping for breath'. In his quest for the French presidency, Michel Barnier pushed decentralisation and the repatriation back to member states of some powers currently exercised at EU level.

National governments do not have to wait for the EU to slow down its slew of harmonising laws. People are still blowing trumpets around the city walls, as Blair put it in 2005. So, governments can and should act immediately to spread power downwards, encouraging initiative from the ground, whether as start-ups or in civil society.

Liberal democracy in the twenty-first century requires genuine commitment to subsidiarity and decentralised decision-making where possible. This is not a zero-sum, binary choice. Deciding the best level for action – local, national or supranational – requires judgement, in tune with the needs of the moment.

Another arguably outdated EU orthodoxy is that the four freedoms are 'indivisible'.

There is no rational basis for grouping together the movement of goods, people, services and capital, other than to sound catchy. In the twenty-first century, doing so is not just arbitrary, it is counterproductive.

The movement of people is fundamentally different to the movement of goods. It affects communities, services and the environment in highly specific ways. And with the ease of travel and modern communications, people are willing to move in numbers never envisaged by drafters of the Treaty, nor even by politicians at the turn of the century.

Large population movements require judgments to be made about solidarity and social security, the adaptability of public services and housing, family breakdown, language provision and left-behind communities – all intensely political issues. Creating an ill-defined concept of EU citizenship, which is then incrementally expanded by the ECJ, in the face of opposition from some member states, is undemocratic and destined to fail. Personally, I am comfortable with quite high levels of legal migration, provided adequate integration follows. Other people are not. Immigration, and peoples' reactions to it, are complex. But it is easy to stoke up hostility and feed people false facts and simple solutions. This makes honest discussion, and considered action, essential.

In recent years, people have begun to see the concept of a borderless world differently. When the Covid virus escaped China, borders went up. This was accepted as the best way to limit its spread and protect populations, ultimately by giving them vaccines.

The Letta report on the single market identifies some of the trade-offs in Schengen. True, much of the inconvenience connected with internal border crossings is gone, but the absence of border control also allows criminal gangs to move more freely (and organise small boat crossings). It is easier to smuggle weapons and drugs and traffic people. Getting to grips with this requires intense co-operation between crime and security agencies across borders and much greater internal policing, including surveillance. The cost of open borders is more intrusive monitoring elsewhere.

Looked at from another perspective, the loss of EU citizenship rights, including the right to live and study (cheaply) in another member state, animates the middle classes in this country like no other issue.

Gisela says she still receives hate mail on this theme, usually from German women. In 2020, before the TCA was concluded, a woman from West Sussex wrote to me. She was furious, she said, that her children's job prospects and studying opportunities had been reduced. Wasn't I concerned that my children had suffered the same? She ended, 'I understand you have had a tough few years with your health and your divorce, but if you have not changed your stance on Brexit, then I hope your next few years continue to be miserable and difficult as they will be for most of the population.' Fortunately for me – though disappointing for my correspondent in West Sussex – they were, at worst, mixed. Still, I did spend some of that time mulling over what she and others feel they – and their children – lost by leaving the EU.

What they have lost is real. However, it ought to be possible to satisfy the aspiration to travel and study in Continental Europe without being bound into a close-knit economic bloc or having to merge political institutions. A mobility pact mooted before the reset, which allows young Europeans to study and work in each other's countries for a limited time, is not the return of free movement as we knew it. It would be a bilateral agreement: if it didn't work it would be up to the parties to change it or scrap it. There is a negotiation to be had over the reciprocal terms – for how long, with what cap on numbers, paying at what rate for a university place. But such a system of exchange, which member states control, should benefit us all.

The ultimate EU orthodoxy concerns the Treaty commitment to 'the process of creating an ever-closer union among the peoples of Europe'. But is 'an ever-closer union' really what the peoples of Europe aspire to, at least outside the eurozone? On the rare occasions they have been asked, they have tended to reject further integration (largely in vain).

In 2013, the Netherlands, a founding member of the EU, declared that the principle of 'ever-closer union' had seen its day. It drew up a table of fifty-four EU measures that would, it said, be better pursued at member-state level.

Might it be wise to find a new formulation, a new aim which reflects the true aspirations of most European citizens and is achievable in practice? Could replacing this aim be a Clause IV moment for the EU, a moment when it redefines what it is for? Think of Tony Blair in 1995, when he jettisoned Clause IV of the Labour Party's constitution, ending its seventy-five-year commitment to public ownership of the means of production. This was seen as a daring move that drew a line in the sand. It set the party on a course of renewal and heralded a decade in power.

So how about replacing 'ever-closer union' with a 'deep and enduring' union? The Treaty would then record that member states were:

> RESOLVED to continue the process of creating a deep and enduring union among the peoples of Europe in which decisions are taken as closely as possible to the citizen in accordance with the principle of subsidiarity.

Because the European Court of Justice is an EU institution (and a motor of greater integration), its role in adjudicating the EU–UK future relationship has been rightly resisted by the UK. Switzerland also took issue with this in its own negotiations with the EU.

The principle that no one should be a judge in their own cause means that an independent arbitrator is needed to adjudicate disputes of this kind. The EU has objected to this because it considers its legal order exceptional, but gradually it seems to be accepting jurisprudential reality.

If the UK (and other countries) were to take part in a more formal trading arrangement with the EU, this could either be overseen by ad hoc arbitration panels or a new court (as envisaged by David Owen), that is not the ECJ. The issue with the ECJ remains the lack of clear limits to its jurisdiction and its practice of interpreting provisions to maximise integration and uniformity.

The question boils down to: who is in charge of the Treaty? The answer has troubled member states other than just the UK. Member states want to retain the ultimate say – but the case law of the ECJ has eaten away at that position. Since the 1970s, the German Constitutional Court has periodically challenged the notion that EU law is superior to all national law, including the German constitution. Germany ratified the Maastricht and Lisbon Treaties, granting the EU institutions greater powers, on the understanding that national governments, parliaments and courts remained 'masters of the Treaties'. Their mastery, however, is at best greatly eroded.

In May 2020, a ruling of Germany's Constitutional Court created a wave of panic in EU legal circles. In a case about eurozone bailout conditions, it refused to follow a decision of the ECJ. The case (Pringle v. Ireland) had provoked weary dismay among jurists and delight among those who believed in preserving the euro at any cost (including by flouting the agreed rules). The German court considered the judgment to be 'simply untenable' and 'objectively arbitrary'. A classic fudge was constructed, bringing the Germans back into line. The French Conseil d'État and the top Czech court have also strained against EU legal supremacy. The tension is unresolved.

Despite the UK's efforts to exit the jurisdiction of the ECJ, the court retains a residual role in Northern Ireland. By agreeing to 'dynamic alignment', the present government would extend that role further. Were the EU member states to take steps to delimit the scope of ECJ jurisdiction by Treaty, this would undoubtedly be welcomed by the UK.

Europe is a rich political, cultural and intellectual mix. And Europe is not just the EU. The UK plays an active part in other vital European organisations. They are not without their challenges, but they form part of our overall engagement with European affairs and our identity as a European nation. In NATO we co-operate with other countries to secure our collective defence. This is pretty much uncontested; indeed (belatedly), we Europeans recognise that we need to do much more. By contrast, disquiet about the Council of Europe, and particularly the ECHR, seems to be mounting.

Present scrutiny of the Convention regime is largely driven by member state concerns about non-EU migration. In May, the leaders of nine EU nations, headed by Denmark and Italy, published an open letter stating that decisions of the Strasbourg court limited their ability to expel 'criminal foreign nationals' and to decide 'how to keep track of them'.

The UK was not a signatory to the letter. In July 2023, days after Keir Starmer took office, he declared full-throated support for the ECHR at a gathering of forty-six European leaders at Blenheim Palace, Churchill's birthplace. Nevertheless, here in the UK, political opposition to the ECHR is hardening. A section of conservative opinion wants to withdraw from it (and presumably from the Council of Europe), also on the basis that the ECHR obstructs robust national measures to curb migration. This is not fact – it is a contention – but it is taking root.

The Council of Europe's secretary general initially rebuffed the nine leaders, suggesting that their intervention risked 'politicising the court'. This is difficult territory. Decisions about human rights – especially on the margins – can be innately political, and so, of course, they matter to governments. Sometimes, the court will step back and say that the issue is one for national authorities. Other times it is criticised for not doing so. Some criticisms, about expansive interpretation, resemble those I have made about the Luxembourg court. I have sympathy with these anxieties, but only up to a point.

I believe that a supranational court that supervises

how governments across Europe (including Russia and Belarus, until their expulsion in February 2022) protect their citizens' human rights is a good thing. Seriously problematic decisions are rare. The legal order is less intrusive than the EU's: judgments of the Strasbourg court do not automatically change national law, and in practice they are implemented through negotiation and compromise. The court's case law doesn't bind national courts, although they are required to take it into account. And notwithstanding the secretary general's defensive response to the nine leaders, the Strasbourg system is generally receptive to dialogue and change.

Opinion on Strasbourg risks dividing into two starkly polarised camps. A government committed to the ECHR should work to reconcile them. The UK is a respected presence in the Council of Europe and its skill at building alliances, brokering agreements and drafting treaties are put to good use there. It is well placed to help ensure that issues raised are fairly addressed, and to work with others to reform the system so that it retains the support it deserves.

The UK has done enough leaving. On this, at a time when our democratic values and institutions are under real pressure, we should be leading.

Liberal democracy has not triumphed over all other systems. Indeed, the world in 2025 is more hostile to it than it was in the 1990s. Crowing about winning the Cold War was foolish. On the other hand, despite what authoritarians such as Xi and Putin like to say, Western liberalism hasn't failed, either.

We do, however, remain prone to complacency. This makes us vulnerable. Think of Europe's reliance on the US security guarantee, or Germany pressing ahead with the Nord Stream gas pipeline in the face of Putin's mounting belligerence. The European project (and leaders) can't be voted from office, and responsibility for decisions can be difficult to locate. This makes it especially liable to wishful thinking and sticking with approaches that no longer work.

Tony Blair's words to the European Parliament in the aftermath of referenda rejecting the Constitutional Treaty are still pertinent today:

> This is not a time to accuse those who want Europe to change of betraying Europe. It is a time to recognise that only by change will Europe recover its strength, its relevance, its idealism and therefore its support amongst the people.

A more perfect union – between the UK and EU, and within Europe more widely – requires vision and change. Taking control of that change, by deliberate, thought-through reform, is vastly preferable to responding to crisis. People have good cause to feel insecure and under threat. Extremists – who do not value the system of liberal democracy we have constructed – will exploit that. But people are less passive and foolish than some choose to believe. In May 2005, Tony Blair seemed to see that as he continued:

> As ever the people are ahead of the politicians. We always think as a political class that people, unconcerned with the daily obsession of politics, may not understand it, may not see its subtleties and complexities. But, ultimately, people always see politics more clearly than us. Precisely because they are not obsessed with it.

Listen to the people, was his exhortation in 2005. Twenty years on, as voters desert the political centre, we need to ramp up the volume on this simple message.

A technological revolution is now underway. To flourish, we need to foster a dynamic economic environment that embraces it wholeheartedly. Advanced democracies will not compete by trying to build walls around old industries (though some may be required for strategic reasons). In years to come, spending on defence, not to mention maintaining the level of social protection that we are accustomed to, will become a serious challenge. We also need to fund protecting the planet and developing clean sources of energy. We can't just load green taxes onto stagnant economies: as the *gilets jaunes* show, people won't accept it and the system will crumble. Bold innovation offers the best chance of achieving all that. There is no point being squeamish about growth.

In the UK, there are heartening signs of a cross-party effort, with former Conservative minister Lord Willetts (encouragingly nicknamed Two Brains) appointed by the Labour government to chair the new Regulatory Innovation Office. Lord Vallance, who led the phenomenally successful vaccine taskforce, is science minister.

This effort is best undertaken in close co-operation with our European partners, but only so far as is compatible with the political model we have chosen: as a self-governing country, open to trade and co-operation with different parts of the world.

Dyson's experience of trying to market an innovative product in the EU shines a light on some of the choices ahead. When safety or technical standards are required, the best forum for this may be international. Regional ones often serve to protect established interests and out-of-date technology and thinking. Institutions – like people – become stale and corrupted. That is natural. So is the need to rethink.

This need to foster innovation feeds into defence, where – for the same reasons and with the same caveat – close collaboration with European partners is to the advantage of all.

As we implement the tech revolution and ramp up our security commitment, we have an opportunity to rethink how the state works. The Blair/Hague report on innovation is not alone in urging that new technology should be harnessed to deliver public services more efficiently and less expensively, not least in the medical sector. Recrafting the state means rethinking how it interacts with citizens: using AI and tech to do simpler tasks, saving the (more expensive) human touch for when it is needed. We have not yet got that right. But here is a generational opportunity that we must grab.

A key feature of a healthy democracy is its ability to discuss and debate. Our adversarial system rests on the belief that a contest between opposing sides – whether in court or in Parliament – is the surest route to the truth or to good solutions. The competition of ideas has a noble track record. But if we are to stay sane, in a world of mass, instantaneous communication, we have to dial down the venom. We need to be able to talk to people with whom we disagree. Rightly, there is alarm over big tech algorithms stoking outrage on social media. Yet the old media also feed off a crisis, a scandal and a political downfall. They too ratchet up the emotion. As ever, we avoid voicing dissent for fear of being swept away by an intolerant tide.

The EU recognises what it calls its 'democratic deficit' – a weak link with the people it aspires to represent. Periodically it comes up with new ways to try to address this, perhaps by granting the European Parliament greater powers (or the Parliament tries to fashion them itself, as with the seemingly defunct *Spitzenkandidaten* process).

None of this addresses the root of the problem. Members of the European Parliament are indeed voted in, but turnout at European elections is low. The people involved can tell themselves that they represent the citizens of Europe, but if those citizens have no idea who they are or what their institution is doing, if they have no opportunities to speak together or meet, it is democracy only in form, not true representation. Europe still lacks a convincing sense of political community – a demos.

Here in the UK, we carry blame for this too. Many people and bodies still mourn our exit from the EU. The BBC, an institution I admire, is probably one. Yet in 2012 – at a time when Europe was an important issue domestically, it took its only programme dedicated entirely to EU politics – *The Record Europe* – off the air. If a public broadcaster doesn't report the workings of a political project to the people, how can the people be expected to understand and identify with it?

Similarly in 2004 the Blair government changed the national curriculum so that modern languages were no longer compulsory at GCSE. Is it any wonder that the UK had so few French-speakers capable of working in EU institutions? If we want to strengthen our links with European political culture, we will need to think how to support that on the ground.

The EU's four freedoms – aiming for the free circulation of goods, services, people and capital – are all very well. But the foundation of freedom, the most fundamental part of our political inheritance, I would argue, is our democracy. This is the pillar supporting all we have built.

Democracy requires participation. Unless people trust in the institutions that govern them, they will fight them

– donning a fluorescent vest and lobbing rocks at police. If they trust the system, they will support it, they will engage, and our political culture will flourish.

Back in the pandemic, I joined thousands of grounded airline staff, lighting engineers, lonely students stranded in London and other miscellaneous volunteers to help administer vaccines. We trained in the deserted tower blocks of Canary Wharf, pumping the chests of mannequins, overseen by St John Ambulance staff. When our unit was ready we jabbed needles in arms, day in day out, in east London's Excel centre, then the Stratford shopping centre. It was a common endeavour that drew together an implausible array of humanity, all of whom – myself included – found it rewarding.

Participation is a strange, nearly magical thing. In the UK, jury service is a civic duty that all citizens may be required to perform. I know many people who have been randomly called up. All report feeling that they had done something meaningful. It can be very difficult, but it feels important, and it is.

In her small book, *The Vitality of Democracy*, Gisela Stuart warns against settling 'for a managed decline' of our political institutions. Rather, she urges us to 'accept individual responsibility for renewing those elements that have fallen into disrepair'. Systems like ours, she points out, don't automatically regenerate themselves: 'Their vitality and legitimacy do not spring from supranational institutions but from the daily interactions of every single one of us.'

My own daily interactions still feature Martin, my colleague and giver-of-the-blue-Euro-mug. He knows I am writing about Europe. I tell him I am reimagining the European Project in a form in which we, the UK, could play a future role. Realising I am not recanting as he had hoped, he is visibly torn between being encouraging (he is, after all, my friend) and being snide. Is she doing something good, he wonders, or something truly awful?

'Europe is my home.' Alessandra's words, spoken over dinner in Milan, express something many of my friends and family feel. These are not citizens of nowhere – to recall Theresa May's jibe in 2016. For different reasons and in different ways, they feel European. Not exclusively, but enough to see themselves as citizens of Europe.

I don't support the legal construct of EU citizenship that we had before – something defined at EU level and policed from the top-down. Rights granted by the EU (after inadequate or non-existent consultation) but delivered, and paid for, by the member states. Citizenship involves give and take. How precisely the social contract works – its benefits and burdens – needs to be worked out, sometimes fought out, via a national political process.

The unhappy mother who wrote to me had a valid point. I do want the next generation to have the chance to travel and live abroad (though maybe parents who have the means will have to pay for it). I don't think the boys who chanted about loving the EU were expressing affection for remote, centralised decision-making. I think they wanted the unfettered freedom to travel, study and later work on the Continent and to see themselves as 'European'.

The mobility pact – referred to by the Government as the 'youth experience scheme', for fear of scaring voters – needs to be developed, consulted widely. People will only call it a return to free movement if no one bothers to explain why it's not.

There are so many things we can do together, and ways we can cooperate, without being in a tight union that weakens our political institutions and democracy. But working together will require greater mutual respect and understanding.

Truth be told, within the EU we were very often fighting. As Wall points out in *Reluctant European*, the first ten years were spent challenging the unfair cost of membership. While crediting Thatcher with some notable achievements, Wall says the pattern of relations she established with the EU usually involved a battle. As the momentum for integration gathered speed, we would fight to secure 'safeguards', then lament as they evaporated before our eyes. One way or another, Europe was always presented as a problem (interfering, uncompetitive) that we – the UK – would fix.

Within the EU, some like-minded member states, were content to hide behind the UK's stand. Others considered that the UK held back the greater integration they sought.

A more perfect union is a more flexible arrangement,

where states that want to integrate closely can, but other looser relationships are also catered for. And it is a structure that respects subsidiarity and recognises that democracies govern for all the people. Government that is too remote cannot adequately represent its citizens and it cannot be held properly to account.

If preserving liberal democracy is the aim, we have to shake off our complacency. In Lampedusa's nineteenth-century novel *The Leopard*, as the Italian *Resorgimento* overturns the old order, Tancredi declares to his uncle the Prince of Salina, 'If we want things to stay as they are, things will have to change.' So, it is now. If we wish to secure our freedom, peace and prosperity, we can no longer stick to the old ways.

The international order is being remade around us. China is busy developing new security structures, like the Global Security Initiative. It is building alternative financial institutions, like the Asian Infrastructure Investment Bank, and working to replace the banking network Swift with its own Cross-border Interbank Payment System (CIPS). It seeks a more 'just and reasonable' order, it says; one less dominated by the US and its allies.

China no longer operates under the radar. It openly sustains Russia's war in Ukraine and asserts a doctrine of great power interests. Mark Rutte, NATO's Secretary-General, may be alarmist when he postulates that if Xi decided to take Taiwan, Putin would invade Europe as a distraction. But the anxiety is real.

In this insecure world, the EU needs better and

more durable relationships with neighbouring countries; relationships that rely less on bullying and more on cooperation in pursuit of common objectives. The UK's strength in defense, intelligence and diplomacy make it an essential strategic ally for the EU, working closely with other large regional powers, France, Germany and Poland.

Both sides need to change gear mentally and stop sulking – the EU could now safely hold off punishing the UK for leaving the club. The UK, for its part, might quit lamenting the choice its voters made in 2016.

A more perfect union is only possible if both sides have the courage to face up to their own imperfections and create something new – letting go of orthodoxies that are outdated and embracing principles promised, but never put into effect:

- Subsidiarity: choose the best level or levels for action – local, national, EU, international – which requires bodies to resist seeking to constantly enhance their own power;
- The ECJ: define – and so limit – the court's jurisdiction by Treaty;
- Concentric circles: create different, mutually agreed arrangements between the EU and its neighbours, which are neither 'one-size-fits-all', nor an inevitable route towards membership;
- The four freedoms: recognise that the free movement of people requires separate consideration from

the other four freedoms, in close consultation with citizens affected by it;

- Ever-closer union: reconsider the aspirations of twenty-first-century Europeans so as to balance better integration with national feeling.

The outcome may not resemble any existing single model, and that is fine.

In leaving the EU, the UK has regained its sovereignty as a self-governing nation. This is a step towards ensuring we are a well-governed nation, but to get there, much more needs to be done. This includes embracing innovation and rethinking how public services are delivered and funded. And it requires finding a greater consensus on migration, asylum and the legal movement of people, decentralising power, and fostering community and communities.

Being a self-governing nation does not mean being insular or closed to the world – that has never been Britain's way. Unshackled, Britain should remain committed to free trade and engaged in creating coalitions to find peaceful solutions to global problems, while upholding the core principles – democracy and the rule of law – that govern our way of life.

Change is happening. Let's mould that change – as agents, not passive victims. And, as far as we can, let's do it together.

Bibliography

Books

Daron Acemoglu and James A. Robinson, *Why Nations Fail*, Profile Books, 2012

Ed. Albertina Albors-Llorens, Catherine Barnard and Brigitte Leucht, *Cassis de Dijon, 40 Years On*, Hart, 2021

Benedict Anderson, *Imagined Communities: Reflections on the Origin and Spread of Nationalism*, Verso, 1991

Anne Applebaum, *Twilight of Democracy: The Failure of Politics and the Parting of Friends*, Penguin, 2021

Catherine Ashton, *And Then What? Inside Stories of 21st Century Diplomacy*, Elliott & Thompson, 2023

Stefan Auer, *Liberal Nationalism in Central Europe*, Routledge Curzon, 2004

Catherine Barnard, *The Substantive Law of the EU*, Oxford University Press, 4th edition, 2014 and 7th edition, 2022

Michel Barnier, trans. Robin Mackay, *My Secret Brexit Diary*, Polity Press, 2021

Lewis Baston, *Borderlines: A History of Europe in 29*

Borders, Hodder Press, 2024

Torsten Bell, *Great Britain? How We Get Our Future Back*, The Bodley Head, 2024

Sylvie Bermann, *Goodbye Britannia, Le Royaume-Uni au défi du Brexit*, Stock, 2021

Ed. Andrea Biondi, Piet Eeckhout and Stefanie Ripley, *EU Law after Lisbon*, Oxford University Press, 2012

Tony Blair, *On Leadership: Lessons for the 21st Century*, Penguin, 2024

Andy Burnham and Steve Rotheram, *Head North: A Rallying Cry for a More Equal Britain*, Trapeze, 2024

Christopher Clark, *Revolutionary Spring: Fighting for a New World 1848–1849*, Allen Lane, 2023

Jason Cowley, *Who are We Now? Stories of Modern England*, Picador, 2022

Ed. Philip Cunliffe, George Hoare, Lee Jones and Peter Ramsay, *Taking Control: Sovereignty and Democracy after Brexit*, Polity Press, 2023

Norman Davies, *Heart of Europe: A Short History of Poland*, Clarendon Press, 1984

Larry Elliott and Dan Atkinson, *Europe Isn't Working*, Yale University Press, 2016

Jonathan Fenby, *The History of Modern France: From the Revolution to the War on Terror*, Simon & Schuster, 2015

Peter Foster, *What Went Wrong with Brexit and What We Can Do About It*, Canongate, 2023

Francis Fukuyama, *Liberalism and its Discontents*, Farrar, Straus and Giroux, 2022

Timothy Garton Ash, *Homelands: A Personal History of Europe*, The Bodley Head, 2023

Stella Ghervas, *Conquering Peace: From the Enlightenment to the European Union*, Harvard University Press, 2021

David Goodhart, *The Road to Somewhere: The Populist Revolt and the Future of Politics*, Hurst & Company, 2017

Brigitte Granville, *What Ails France?*, McGill-Queen's University Press, 2021

Dina Gusejnova, *European Elites and Ideas of Empire, 1917–1957*, Cambridge University Press, 2016

Daniel Hannan, *What Next: How to get the best from Brexit*, Head of Zeus, 2016

TC Hartley, *The Foundations of European Union Law*, Oxford University Press, 8th edition, 2014

Katja Hoyer, *Beyond the Wall: East Germany 1949–1990*, Allen Lane, 2023

Andrew Hussey, *The French Intifada: The Long War Between France and Its Arabs*, Granta, 2014

Julian Jackson, *A Certain Idea of France: The Life of Charles de Gaulle*, Penguin, 2019

Tony Judt, *A Grand Illusion? An Essay on Europe*, New York University Press, 2011

——— *Postwar: A History of Europe since 1945*, Vintage Books, 2010

John Kampfner, *Why the Germans do it Better: Notes from a Grown-Up Country*, Atlantic Books, 2020

Kapka Kassabova, *Border: A Journey to the Edge of Europe*, Granta, 2017

Ivan Krastev and Stephen Holmes, *The Light that Failed: A Reckoning*, Allen Lane, 2019

Jarosław Kuisz, *The New Politics of Poland: A Case of Post-traumatic Sovereignty*, Manchester University Press, 2023

Hans Kundnani, *Eurowhiteness: Culture, Empire and Race in the European Project*, Hurst & Company, 2023

Neil MacGregor, *Germany: Memories of a Nation*, Allen Lane, 2014

David McKittrick and David McVea, *Making Sense of the Troubles*, Viking, 2012

Margaret MacMillan, *The Uses and Abuses of History*, Profile Books, 2010

——— *War: How Conflict Shaped Us,* Profile Books, 2020

——— *The War That Ended Peace*, Profile Books, 2014

James Madison, Alexander Hamilton and John Jay, *The Federalist Papers*, Penguin Classics, 1987

Geert Mak, *The Dream of Europe: Travels in the 21st Century*, Harvill Secker, 2021

Jan-Werner Müller, *Democracy Rules*, Allen Lane, 2021

Wolfgang Münchau, *Kaput: The End of the German Miracle*, Swift, 2024

David Owen, *Europe Restructured: The Eurozone Crisis and its Aftermath,* Methuen, 2012

Sophie Pedder, *Revolution Française: Emmanuel Macron and the Quest to Reinvent a Nation*, Bloomsbury Continuum, 2019

Ed. Steve Peers, Tamara Hervey, Jeff Kenner and Angela Ward, *The EU Charter of Fundamental Rights: A Commentary*, Hart Publishing, 2014

Jonathan Powell, *Great Hatred, Little Room: Making Peace in Northern Ireland*, Vintage Books, 2009

Stein Ringen, *The Story of Scandinavia: From the Vikings to Social Democracy*, Weidenfeld & Nicolson, 2023

Amartya Sen, *Identity and Violence: The Illusion of Destiny*, W. W. Norton & Company, 2006

Tim Shipman, *Fall Out: A Year of Political Mayhem*, Willam Collins, 2017

Rory Stewart, *Politics on the Edge*, Vintage, 2023

Lawrence Stone, *The Causes of the English Revolution 1529–1642*, Routledge, 2001

Gisela Stuart, *The Vitality of Democracy*, Haus, 2022

Colm Tóbín, *Bad Blood: A Walk Along the Irish Border*, Picador, 2010

Robert Tombs, *This Sovereign Isle: Britain In and Out of Europe*, Allen Lane, 2021

Giles Tremlett, *Ghosts of Spain: Travels Through a Country's Hidden Past*, Faber & Faber, 2012

Richard Tuck, *The Left Case for Brexit: Reflections on the Current Crisis*, Polity Press, 2020

Yanis Varoufakis, *And the Weak Suffer What They Must?*, Vintage, 2017

Stephen Wall, *Reluctant European: Britain and the European Union from 1945 to Brexit*, Oxford University Press, 2020

Shirin Wheeler, *Charles Wheeler: Witness to the Twentieth*

Century, Manilla Press, 2023

Lea Ypi, *Free: Coming of Age at the End of History*, Penguin, 2021

Adam Zamoyski, *Poland: A History*, William Collins, 2009

—————— *Napoleon: A Life*, Basic Books, 2018

Reports

HMG

Prime Minister Statement on EU Renegotiation: 3 February 2016

HM Treasury analysis: the immediate economic impact of leaving the EU, May 2016 Cm 9292

Global Britain in a Competitive Age: the Integrated Review of Security, Defense, Development and Foreign Policy, March 2021

Integrated Review Refresh 2023, HMG, CP811

The Windsor Framework: A new way forward, February 2023, CP 806

The UK Strategic Defense Review 2025, Ministry of Defense

EU

Draft Decisions of the Heads of State or Government, meeting within the European Council, concerning a New Settlement for the United Kingdom within the European Union, 2 February 2016 (EUCO 4/16)

White Paper on the Future of Europe, European Commission, March 2017

OLAF European Anti-Fraud Office Investigation Report into Frontex and Executive Director, Fabrice Leggeri (Olaf.03(2021)21088), October 2022

Mario Draghi, *The Future of European Competitiveness*, September 2024

Enrico Letta, *Much More Than a Market*, Empowering the Single Market to deliver a sustainable future and prosperity for all EU citizens, April 2024

Sailing on High Seas: Reforming and Enlarging the EU for the 21st Century, Report of the Franco-German Working Group on EU Institutional Reform, 2023

Independent Reports

Richard Ekins, Jonathan Morgan, Tom Tugendhat, *Clearing the Fog of Law: Saving our armed forces from defeat by judicial diktat*, Policy Exchange, 2015

Tony Blair and William Hague, *A New National Purpose: Innovation Can Power the Future of Britain*, Tony Blair Institute for Global Change, 2023

David Willetts, *The Eight Great Technologies 10 years on, An Industrial Strategy*, Policy Exchange, 2023

Centre for European Reform (CER) Reports

Clara Marina O'Donnell, *The trials and tribulations of European defence co-operation*, July 2013

Hugo Brady, *Twelve things everyone should know about the European Court of Justice*, July 2014

Sander Tordoir, Aslak Berg, Elisabetta Cornago, Zach Meyers and Luigi Scazzieri, *Draghi's plan to rescue the European economy: Will EU leaders do whatever it takes?*, September 2024

Anton Spisak, *The new EU–Swiss deal: What it means and the lessons it holds for the UK–EU "reset"*, 17 March 2025

Luigi Scazzieri, *How the UK and the EU can deepen defence co-operation*, March 2025

Aslak Berg, Ian Bond and Charles Grant, *Not a summit of ambition*, 12 May 2025

Ian Bond, *NATO Summit 2025: Time to build a proper European Pillar?* 2 June 2025

Martin Donnelly, *The next steps for the UK–EU reset*, 19 June 2025

Independent Reports

Brussels News, Newsletter for the Bar Council of England and Wales, Brussels Representation Office (various)

Dr Nicolai von Ondarza, Johanna Flach, Max Becker, *Resetting UK–EU defence cooperation: the case for a special partnership*, UK in a Changing Europe, 18 March 2022

Judgments

R (on the application of Miller and Dos Santos) v Secretary of State for Exiting the European Union [2017] UKSC 5, [2018] AC 61 on appeal from [2016] EWHC 2768 (Admin)

R (on the application of Miller) v The Prime Minister [2019] UKSC 41 on appeals from (Divisional Court) [2019] EWHC 2381 (QB) and [2019] CSIH 49

Case 6/64 *Costa v ENEL* [1964] ECR 585

Case 41/74 *Van Duyn v Home Office* [1974] ECR 1337

Case C-120/78 *Rewe Zentral AG v Bundesmonopolverwaltung fur Branntwein* (Cassis de Dijon) [1979] ECR 649

Cases C-293/12 and C-594/12 *Digital Rights Ireland Ltd v Minister for Communications, Marine and natural Resources & others and Seitlinger and Others* [2015] 1 QB 127; [2014] 3 CMLR 44

Opinion 2/13 (Full Court) [2014] ECR I-2454

Case C-370/12 *Thomas Pringle v Government of Ireland* ECLI:EU:C:2012:756

Case T-544/13 *Dyson Ltd v European Commission* [2018] EUECJ T-544/13RENV

Articles

[*these are placed in the order in which they are referred to in the text*]

Julian Coman, 'Michel Barnier: Why is the EU's former Brexit chief negotiator sounding like a Eurosceptic?', *Observer*, 26.09.2021

'Brexit: British expats sue EU's Juncker over talks', *BBC online*, 07.10.16

Daniel Hannan, 'Almost any MEP in Brussels could be prosecuted. Only Eurosceptics like Le Pen are', *Daily Telegraph*, 05.04.2025

Boris Johnson, 'EC hand reaches out to the grave', *Daily Telegraph*, 25.02.1992

Boris Johnson, 'Threat to British Pink Sausages', *Daily Telegraph*, 14.10.1992

David Trimble, 'EU Intransigence threatens the Good Friday agreement', *The Times*, 10.06.2021

'They're back', *The Economist*, 07.06.2025

Wolfgang Münchau, 'Starmer's "EU reset" is a fairytale. There will be no sunny uplands', *Unherd*, 19.05.2025

Francois-Joseph Schichan, 'Restore friendly ties with the EU but don't backtrack on Brexit', *The Times*, 15.05.2025

Rohan Silva, 'We can't let EU's anti-AI rules drag us down too', *The Times*, 19.08.2024

Peter Foster and Madeleine Speed, 'How UK regulators are missing the chance to make the best of Brexit', *Financial Times*, 27.02.2024

Enrico Letta, 'There is no other London – it can still be the financial capital of Europe', *Observer*, 19.05.2025

Speeches / misc

Memorandum of Conference with President Eisenhower, 04.11.1959, Office of the Historian

Margaret Thatcher, 'The Bruges Speech' to the College of Europe, 20.09.1988

Tony Blair, Speech to the European Parliament, Strasbourg, 26.10.2005

Radoslaw Sikorski, speaking to Allianz Forum, Berlin, 28.11.2011

David Cameron, Speech to Bloomberg HQ, London, 23.01.2013

Philippe Sands QC lecture at European Society of International Lawyers (ESIL), Oslo, 'Developments in Geopolitics – the End(s) of Judicialization?' 12.09.2015

Jean-Claude Juncker, Speech to European Parliament, Brussels, 28.06.2016

Podcasts

The Ezra Klein Show, 'The Breaking of the Constitutional Order', The New York Times Podcasts, 05.02.2025

Tom Holland and Dominic Sandbrook, *The Rest is History*, Goalhanger, various

Acknowledgements

This book is the fruit of discussion, and dispute, with numerous different people over an extended period. I am grateful to you all for enriching my understanding and for engaging with me on a tricky, fraught, but important subject.

Some of you have had a direct input into the text and for your insights I thank you warmly. I also thank those of you who gave me contacts, rummaged around to find old lecture notes and articles, or generously responded to my questions despite it being many years since we had spoken last.

I'd like to pay special tribute to my former colleagues at Stanbrook & Hooper, European Community Lawyers (as it was), to the late Clive Stanbrook QC, who gave me my first job on the Rue du Taciturne, in Brussels, and to Catriona and Jacqueline, friends who remain dedicated to the European Project and who stood with me recently outside the Berlaymont Building, as I ruminated. Thanks also to Federico Bianchi at the EU Delegation to the UK.

My mediation and psychology colleagues, I thank

you, too, for your vital work helping me (inadvertently perhaps) to cultivate enough detachment to return to this bruising topic and better understand the problems we face.

Thanks to all who agreed to read, and helpfully commented on, the draft text: my friends Wendy Outhwaite KC, Conrad Roeber, Nell Butler, Lucy Kellaway, Gillian Kettaneh; my son Theo Johnson-Wheeler; and my American godmother, Jenonne Walker. Baroness (Gisela) Stuart, reader of a mildly more polished version, provided sound and welcome advice, for which I am hugely grateful. Any errors are, of course, my responsibility alone.

Heartfelt thanks to my agent, Gordon Wise at Curtis Brown, for your continuing support and guidance, and for your hard work on my behalf.

The energetic team at Weidenfeld & Nicolson did me proud. My editor, Ed Lake, picked up this project, helped shape it and was instrumental in bringing it to fruition. Thank you for doing so with discernment and good humour. And thanks to Jo Roberts-Miller and Elizabeth Allen for your dedication and professionalism.

Thanks finally to my late parents, Charles and Dip, for pretty much everything.

About the Author

Marina Wheeler is a noted KC, specialising in public and human rights law. She was born in West Berlin and educated in Brussels, at the heart of the European Project. For twenty-five years she was married to Boris Johnson, and was in the room when many of the key Brexit discussions took place. She recently turned her hand to mediation.